THE PUZZLE

Dr Peter Vardy lectures in Philosophy of Religion at Heythrop College, University of London. He is author of the best-selling *Puzzle* series of books (now published in Britain, Australia, the United States, Holland, Poland and Germany) and series editor of the *Fount Christian Thinkers* series. Dr Vardy is Course Director of the University of London's External BD programme, and a former Chair of the University's Board of Theological Studies. He and his wife Anne have five children.

Praise for Peter Vardy's *The Puzzle of Sex*:

'*The Puzzle of Sex*' brings together in a deft, fascinating and easily accessible manner understandings of human sexuality based on current biblical scholarship, the insights and beliefs of different traditions, psychology and ethical discussion and argument. Traditional moral arguments are critically evaluated and current issues are clarified in a way that helps the reader come to a more mature assessment of their own views on this critical area of human experience.'
BRENDAN CALLAGHAN SJ, Psychology of Religion, University of London

'Peter Vardy has the gift of making philosophy and theology lively and relevant to contemporary experience. He has provided a timely and provocative discussion of sexual ethics and an invaluable source of reflection. *The Puzzle of Sex* should become standard reading for A-level students and is a book which deserves a wide audience.'
JEREMY HALL, EDITOR, *Dialogues*

The Puzzle of Sex

PETER VARDY

Fount
An Imprint of HarperCollins*Publishers*

Fount Paperbacks is an Imprint of
HarperCollins *Religious*
Part of HarperCollins *Publishers*
77–85 Fulham Palace Road, London W6 8JB

First published in Great Britain
in 1997 by Fount Paperbacks

3 5 7 9 10 8 6 4 2

A catalogue record for this book is
available from the British Library

ISBN 0 00 628042 0

Printed and bound in Great Britain by
Caledonian International Book Manufacturing Ltd,
Glasgow

Contents

ACKNOWLEDGEMENTS

My thanks are due to many friends who have shared their personal journeys with me over the years, but, in particular, I am grateful to the following who read and criticized early drafts (or sometimes individual chapters) of the manuscript. The errors are all my own, but there would have been more of them without their help: Brendan Callaghan SJ; Catherine Cowley; Judy Grill; Valerie Holmes; Bernard Hoose; Paul Kefford; Frances King; Felicity McCutcheon; Richard Price; Bridget Upton; Anne, Catherine and Kirsten Vardy. This book would not have been written without the suggestion of Professor Ian Markham, who, in a review of an earlier book written by Paul Grosch and I on *The Puzzle of Ethics*, suggested this title. I am grateful for the helpful and intelligent copy-editing of Thomas Allain-Chapman.

PETER VARDY
Heythrop College
University of London
Ash Wednesday 1997

Introduction

All human beings are sexual creatures and there are few, if any, for whom the whole area of sexuality and relationships is not of interest and concern. This book starts by taking seriously theological reflection about sex from the perspective of the Hebrew Scriptures and the New Testament. Immediately some will ask, 'Why bother with this? I am not a Christian, so this is of no relevance to my thinking on sexual ethics.' This is an understandable position, but Western ideas have emerged from a Judaeo-Christian culture and if one is to understand current views on sex one has to trace their origins. Unless we understand where existing ideas have come from, we will not be able to develop a rational way forward.

It will be suggested in this book that the time has come for a reappraisal of traditional views on sexual ethics. Such a reappraisal will, of course, be resisted as every other reappraisal has been resisted, but counter arguments then need to be presented taking account of the known evidence including that gleaned from genetics, psychology and the physical sciences. Some hold that sexual morality is set in stone and can never alter but, as this book will make clear, this is far from the case.

To claim that the time has come for a change in traditional sexual ethics is to suggest that we have reached a turning point and that to continue with old understandings is to fail to be truthful. There have been many such turning points in the history of thinking about human beings in relation to God and the whole moral order:

Introduction

1   The Book of Job is an account of how one man's experience of, and reflection on, the problem of innocent suffering led him to reject the then accepted view that those who did well in the world were loved by God and whoever suffered had in some way offended God. Job refused to accept this and the book which bears his name is a record of the struggle to come to grips with the inadequacy of the prevailing ideas about suffering, in the face of opposition from his closest friends.

2   The Book of Jonah, written after the restoration of the City of Jerusalem and the long years of exile in Babylon, records the rejection of the insular theological attitude of Israel's prophets who saw God as their own God who was not concerned with any other nations of the world. Jonah refused to prophesy repentance to the great but heathen city of Ninevah – because he thought they might actually repent and thereby be saved from destruction. Eventually God forced Jonah to Ninevah and the story unfolds showing that Israel's God is God of the whole world and concerned with all people, totally contrary to the prevailing view held by many Israelites.

3   St Augustine of Hippo, writing at the time when the Roman empire had just become Christian, reflecting on Jesus' teaching that one should forgive one's enemies and never do harm to those who harmed you, came to the realization that warfare was permissible to Christians provided the cause was just. Up to his time, most Christians had been pacifists yet Augustine claimed that this understanding was inadequate and this has changed the whole subsequent way war was regarded.

4   St Thomas Aquinas supported the feudal system in society including the idea of slaves. Slavery was accepted by the Church and it took Christians like Wilberforce to overturn the conventional wisdom and to reach a new and higher level of understanding of the essential brother and sisterhood of all human beings.

5   Luther, after being himself a monk, reflected on the state of the Christian Church and came to reject significant parts of commonly accepted practices in the Church – particularly concerning the practice of selling 'indulgences'. He was condemned and persecuted but he arrived at new insights and, in time, different Churches came to see the merit of many of his views.

6   The conquistadors of Spain brought disease, slavery, torture and degradation to millions in South America in the name of Christianity and in their greed for gold. The British empire built part of its prosperity on the slave trade and the denial of the humanity of 'blacks'. The Calvinism of the Afrikaners built their security on apartheid and the subjugation of non-white South Africans. It took the pioneering work of Oscar Romero, Martin Luther King, Trevor Huddlestone, Nelson Mandela, and many others to maintain the fundamental equality of all human beings, often in opposition to established Churches.

7   The Reformation overturned a long Western Church tradition and Protestant Churches allowed married clergy – as the Orthodox Church has always done. The Roman Catholic Church has yet to follow the same path but already Anglican and Lutheran married priests who convert to being Roman Catholics are being conditionally 're-ordained' and are then recognized as Catholic priests.

8   The Catholic Church taught, until comparatively recently, that, following Aristotle, God implanted a soul in a male foetus at 40 days and in a female foetus at 90 days. Someone who caused a miscarriage or who performed an abortion prior to this date was not held to be guilty of murder but only of a minor or venial sin equivalent to the use of contraception. This has been superseded by later teachings which held that a soul was introduced at the moment of conception or even, more recently, that it is impossible to be sure when personhood occurs.

9   The Inquisition handed over to the secular authorities thousands of people to be burnt in order to maintain 'true belief', convinced

that the flames of the pyres would remind people of hell and cause them to repent – most people (although not all) have learnt that freedom of conscience must be respected.

10 Usury or lending money at interest was for centuries an excommunication offence. This was the main reason that Jews were, historically, forced by Christians into being bankers, because only they could lend money at interest to non-Jews without being subject to Church condemnation. Today, people recognize that the old prohibitions against usury related to a time when people were living a hand to mouth existence and it was unacceptable to take as security the basic essentials of life such as a man's coat. In today's more complex world, lending money at interest is now considered acceptable by all Churches even though this is specifically condemned in the Bible.

11 The literal accounts of creation put forward in Genesis were, up to a hundred and fifty years ago, considered an essential article of faith by most Christians, yet Darwin's work on evolution and Lyell's work on geology showed that the creation stories could no longer be taken literally. Most mainstream Christian Churches now accept this and see these stories as depicting the dependence of the universe on God rather than a specific account of events.

In spite of the clear evidence that there have been many significant turning points in ethical and theological debate in the past, some may still say that there is no 'Puzzle of Sex'. Moral teaching is straightforward:

- Sex before marriage is wrong
- Homosexual behaviour is wicked
- Adultery is against the law of God
- Masturbation is a grave sin
- The main purpose of sex is for procreation
- Sex is only acceptable within the marriage of one man and one woman

- A woman has a duty to provide sexual access to a man if she is married to him
- Sex is to be treated with suspicion and as a temptation
- Celibacy is a higher ideal than married life.

This book will argue that none of the above statements are straightforward and that the ethical problems are more complicated and less clear than many assume.

It may be asked at the outset why this book concentrates on the Judaeo-Christian tradition and does not take into account the teachings of that other major monotheistic faith, Islam. This is a fair question – the reason is that one of the central pillars of Islam is that the Holy Qur'ān was dictated to Muhammad by Allah. If this is true, then the teachings of the Qur'ān regarding sex, marriage, divorce and the position of women in society cannot be seriously questioned, even though different parts of the Qur'ān may need to be balanced against each other in some cases. Most Muslims will, of course, maintain the truth of this claim whereas Atheists, Agnostics, Christians and Jews will either reject it or, at least, be doubtful. Given such a divergence of starting points it would be difficult to integrate an Islamic perspective with a developing understanding which appeals to reason and not solely to revelation.

The Idea of Development

Biblical criticism has shown the extent to which the stories of the Bible are radically conditioned by the culture within which they were written – they are stories written by human beings of their own understandings of God's work in history and of what forms of human behaviour are appropriate. Understandings of moral and religious ideas found in the Bible develop over time – as one would expect of any account written by human beings. Scientific understanding of the universe develops with the passage of the years due to new discoveries, so, in a similar way, theological and moral reflection develop over the centuries. As an example, for much of the

Hebrew Scriptures, God is seen in anthropomorphic terms – he is like a great king who arbitrarily chooses favourites, he must be appeased and he can walk on the earth almost like a super-human being. This understanding becomes revised over the years and gradually the realization dawns that even the heaven of heavens cannot contain God. God is not a God who can be found within a moveable Ark, or a Temple or a particular people. God eventually came to be seen no longer as a God of one people but as a God of the whole earth.

This is not to deny continuity between the Hebrew Scriptures and the New Testament – quite the reverse. The continuity provided by the Bible stories lies in the developing understanding about God and how human beings should live together.

This idea of development has not always been accepted. For instance the Roman Catholic Church resisted it – in the First Vatican Council of 1870 there was no sign of any doctrine of development at all, indeed it was specifically rejected in that Council's document entitled 'Constitution on the Catholic Faith'.[1] However, within less than a hundred years, the mood in the Catholic Church had changed, and by the time of the Second Vatican Council in 1965 the idea of development was accepted in the 'Constitution on Divine Revelation', which states:

> The tradition which comes from the Apostles develops in the Church with the help of the Holy Spirit. For there is growth in the understanding of the realities and the words which have been handed down.

This comes about:

> Through the contemplation and study made by believers, who treasure these things in their hearts, through the intimate understanding of spiritual things they experience, and through the

---

[1] Denzinger, 'On Faith and Reason', chapter 4.

preaching of those who have received through episcopal succession the sure gift of truth.

Generally such development is gradual and does not reject what went before. However, there have been many times in the Church's history when the teaching given has been, quite simply, wrong, and it is at least possible that this may now be the case in the sexual realm.

Today there is a greater appreciation of the sophistication of the biblical texts than ever in the past. Our knowledge of philosophy has increased enormously, as has our understanding of human biology and psychology. Even for those who believe in God, it would be surprising if, in the face of this increase in knowledge, our ideas of what constitutes appropriate sexual behaviour remain unchanged – yet all too often this is assumed to be the case. As has been shown, there have been many significant moments when religious and moral ideas have altered and past understandings rejected. This same, it will be argued, now applies in the arena of sexual ethics.

PART 1

HOW WE GOT TO
WHERE WE ARE

ONE
Men and Women:
The Creation Stories

Within European thought, many attitudes towards sexual relationships depend, even if indirectly, on the Bible. Yet the Bible was written by human beings. There is no suggestion in Christianity, Judaism or Islam that the books of the Bible were written other than by human beings who were telling their story of God's interaction with the world. The biblical stories are complex and sophisticated narratives which were given great thought. It is easy to read them far too simplistically.

The same phrases can occur again and again in the biblical accounts, albeit with slight shifts of emphasis in different settings. It is essential, therefore, that the reader of a text should pay attention to the context and should seek to understand what the writer wishes to say. What cannot and must not be done is to take a few words of text out of the context in which they are placed. It is also important to recognize that any reader brings their own presuppositions to bear on the text and these influence interpretation. The idea of anyone having a total lack of presuppositions is nonsense – we are all the products of our experience and our own individual perspectives. We cannot be completely neutral. The biblical accounts have been used in different ways by many groups, often to serve their own interests.

If one is going to try to avoid imposing one's own prior convictions on the biblical material, it is essential to take the text seriously. The more people wish the Bible to 'speak' to them of God, the more they have an obligation to try to understand exactly what the Bible is saying. Nowhere is this more the case than in the area of

3

sexual relations where a few key texts are often quoted out of context and with limited understanding.

The New Testament has surprisingly little to say about sex – and this particularly applies to the Gospels. The Hebrew Scriptures speak of sexual matters in more detail although the relevance of these comments today is a matter for debate. However prior to tackling the specific references to sexual behaviour, a more general theme needs to be dealt with at some length – and that is the relation between men and women. The biblical story of creation is the starting point as it has been highly influential on future relationships between men and women. In addition, Jesus is recorded as drawing on the creation story in support of his views on marriage,[1] whilst some of the epistles recall either Eve's creation or sin.[2]

The Genesis Accounts of Creation

The Hebrew Scriptures contain two creation stories which are entirely separate – they come from two different traditions and two different authors and were placed together long after the original stories were passed down by word of mouth in an oral tradition that would have extended over many centuries.

The first of these stories is contained in Genesis 1:1–2:4a, the second runs from Genesis 2:4 to 2:24. The first story is dated by scholars around the sixth century BCE and was probably written about the time of the Exile into Babylon after the destruction of Jerusalem. The second account is held to be earlier, probably from around 1000 BCE. Both accounts, the one written from a time of disaster, and the earlier written in a time of prosperity, refer to the sexuality of human beings.

The First Creation Story
This story has men and women being created together. The crucial passage is:

[1] Mark 10:1–12, Matthew 19:1–9.
[2] E.g. 1 Corinthians 11:7–9;12, 1 Timothy 2:11–15.

Then God said 'Let us make *man* in our image, after our likeness; and let *them* have dominion over the fish of the sea, and over the birds of the air, and over the cattle, and over all the earth, and over every creeping thing that creeps upon the earth.' So God created *man* in his own image, in the image of God he created him, *male and female* he created them.' (Genesis 1:26–27)

The Hebrew word for 'man' is *adam*. This word means 'human being' and is not specifically gendered – it is an incorrect translation, therefore, to say that 'God created man' – rather, God created human beings. Many misunderstandings have arisen due to a failure to recognize this. God does not first create a male and subsequently a female – he creates male and female together. Both human beings are given dominion over the earth, its plants and its animals. Both are given the same food to eat. In fact, male and female are specifically stated as being in the image of God. God can, thus, be talked of as both male and female,[3] yet either perspective on its own will only capture part of God's reality. God is not a man or a woman (no serious theologian has ever thought that God was), but metaphoric talk of God in male and female terms can help to increase understanding of God.

Once the male and female human beings were created, then the story continues:

God blessed them and said to them 'Be fruitful and multiply, and fill the earth and subdue it; and have dominion over the fish of the sea …' And God saw everything that he had made and, behold, it was very good. (Genesis 1:28;31)

This creation story thus records, right at the beginning, that God created males and females together and blessed them both – their gender, involved in the command to multiply, was part of this

---

[3] There are two biblical passages in which God is specifically referred to in feminine terms – Deuteronomy 32:11 and Jesus' saying in Matthew 23:37.

blessing and is strongly emphasized as good. The whole of the first account of creation is positive and there are no negatives at all. Man and woman are together created by God, together they are blessed, together as part of this blessing they are told to populate the earth and God is pleased with God's handiwork.

The idea of God creating human beings together is echoed later in Genesis:

> When God created man [*adam* – human being], he made him in the likeness of God. Male and female he created them, and he blessed them and named them Man when they were created. (Genesis 5:1b–2)

It is important to notice that it is only human beings whom God *names*. The idea of 'naming' is important – God gives to human beings the power to name animals, but in the case of human beings themselves it is God who gives them the generic name 'Man' which covers both male and female. Human beings are made for each other and are part of the wider whole of creation.

The Second Creation Story
The second Genesis account is inserted after the first, although it was written about four hundred years earlier. It is a completely separate account and gives a different version of creation. No attempt has been made by the early compilers of the written text we now have in front of us to harmonize the two stories – they are left distinct and can be treated as separate accounts. Whereas the first creation story is clear in emphasizing the equality of men and women, the second story appears more ambiguous. 'Adam' is created first and Eve is created subsequent as a 'helpmate'. The woman appears to be in a subservient position and, indeed, some theologians have said that it is by the woman's sin (listening to the temptation of the serpent) that Adam is caused to sin. This reading has given a negative role to women down the centuries – but it is simplistic and largely untrue, as a careful reading of the story makes clear. Indeed the word *adam* is not even a name at all!

In this second story, *adam* (which is wrongly translated in many Bibles as 'man' but in fact means creature of the earth or human being) is not created directly – *adam* is created from the dust of the ground which apparently existed prior to the creation. God then breathes life into this creature. So we have:

> Then the Lord God formed *adam* of dust from the ground, and breathed into his nostrils the breath of life; and *adam* became a living being. (Genesis 2:7)

In this second story, the human being or earth creature is the central focus of God's attention and everything revolves around it. Plants and animals are brought to it for naming and it is placed in a garden watered by a river which divides into four to form the four great rivers of the then known world. *Adam* is given power over all creatures, symbolized by all the creatures being brought before *adam* for naming. However this *adam* does not have a companion – none of the animals are suitable for this role. God, therefore, decides to create a companion or helper for the earth creature.

Phyllis Trible, in her book *God and the Rhetoric of Sexuality* points out that both the words 'companion' and 'helper' have unfortunate connotations in English which do not exist in the original Hebrew. In English, these words imply someone in a subservient position or an assistant. Trible says: 'To the contrary, in the Hebrew Scriptures this word often describes God as the superior who creates and saves Israel.'[4] God is, therefore, described by the same word used to describe *adam*'s helper – the connotation, therefore, is far removed from someone who is inferior. However, the crucial point to understand in relation to human gender is the manner of the creation of male and female from the asexual *adam*.

God creates woman out of *adam*, the earth creature, and, as Trible points out, it is only *after* this creation that *adam* is described as male. The Hebrew word for woman is *issa* and it is only after the

---

[4] Phyllis Trible, *God and the Rhetoric of Sexuality*, Fortress Press, 1978, p. 90.

7

creation of woman that the earth creature is described as *is*, which means man. Thus the verses can be rendered as follows:

> Then the *adam* said, 'This at last is bone of my bones and flesh of my flesh; she shall be called *issa* because she was taken out of *is*.' (Genesis 2:23)

Trible puts the point like this:

> The new creature, built upon the material of *adam*, is female, receiving her identity in a word that is altogether new to the story, the word *issa*. The old creature transformed is male, similarly receiving identity in a word that is new to the story, *is*. (Trible, p. 97)

Male and female are, therefore, created simultaneously out of the non-gendered earth creature. The two human beings are made for each other – there is no suggestion in the text of the male dominating or having superiority over the female. *Adam*, in earlier verses, is given dominion over all animals but no such dominion is given to the male over the female. We have, instead, two equals.

However, the story does not end there. The serpent comes to tempt the first woman and the first woman is portrayed as autonomous, free and able to make her own decisions. In response to the serpent's question, she accurately summarizes God's command to her and her partner not to eat and God's threat of death if they act against God's command. The serpent appeals to her rational powers:

> 'You will not die. For God knows that when you eat of it your eyes will be opened, and you will be like God, knowing good and evil.' (Genesis 3:4–5)

The woman eats the fruit because she saw that it was desirable and it would make her wise – but God's punishment came on her and the man because of their disobedience. She offers the fruit to the man who also ate – there was no suggestion of beguiling, tempting activity by the woman. There were two autonomous individuals who made their own decisions. The man was not criticized for failing to control the woman – he had no right of control.

God is then recorded as punishing the two of them for their disobedience: the man is made to work for a living and the woman will give birth – both of which result in pain – and God ejects them from the garden. However, the truly significant point is that it is only after their punishment by God that man's dominance over woman becomes asserted for the first time. The author of this account has God specifically state that the man will 'rule over' the woman (Genesis 3:16). As a result of this, the man now *names* his wife Eve (3:20) – this is significant because it is the act of naming which confers control. God brought the animals to *adam* so that he could name them, and this naming constituted his dominance. When the man now names the woman he asserts, for the first time, his dominance over her, and reduces her to much the same status as the animals which he already controls.

Lisa Cahill says that '... we find that supremacy and subordination, as distinct from difference and co-operation, are not part of the original creation but of the condition of sin ... man and woman have equal responsibility and dignity'.[5] In other words, the idea of male supremacy and female obedience is only introduced in the second account as a result of the disorder brought about by sin.

The Two Creation Stories Contrasted
Several points should be clear from the above:

1 There are two entirely distinct stories of creation which cannot easily be harmonized although it is true that the two accounts are recorded alongside each other.

[5] Lisa Cahill, *Between the Sexes: Foundations for a Christian Ethic of Sexuality*, Fortress Press, 1985, p. 56.

9

2 These stories were written by human beings who reflected on God's creative and sustaining activity in the world.

3 Both the stories have men and women being created absolutely equal, although in the second story woman becomes subservient after the Fall. These accounts do not pretend to be divinely dictated – they are stories portraying the dependence of the universe on God and contain great insight and wisdom, but they were written by human beings a long time after the events they purport to describe and are human reflections on the relationship of God to the world.

Today we live in a culture where women are recognized as autonomous human beings, able to make decisions in their own right. It must be acknowledged, however, that for thousands of years women have not been looked at in this way – all too often, women have been regarded as possessions with men exercising rights of ownership over them. F. X. Murphy points out:

> A misogynistic and patriarchal prejudice has pervaded the Church's moral thought down the ages, based on the incident of Eve as the temptress in Genesis, and confirmed by the Stoic rhetoric in which the early Christian thinkers were trained ... Churchmen from Tertullian and Cyprian in the third century to Jerome and John Chrysostom in the fifth, delighted in denigrating womanhood as the source of the human race's downfall.[6]

As we shall see, the story of Eve's temptation of Adam was one of the foundation stones on which Christian theologians and leaders have built their understanding of sexuality and God's will for the relationship between men and women, and, in particular, the subservient position of women. It is a position which can no longer be justified.

---

[6] F. X. Murphy, 'Of Sex and the Catholic Church', *Atlantic Monthly*, February 1981, p. 44.

TWO

The Ten Commandments

The Ten Commandments are of vital importance in the developing understanding of human relationships and the approach to sexuality, although their importance has often been overstressed and they have been read selectively and with the interests of the readers in mind. The story of the giving of the Ten Commandments by God to Moses and then to the people of Israel marked the third covenant between God and human beings. The first covenant was God's promise to Noah that never again would rain be used to wipe out humanity and the symbol of this was the rainbow.[1] The second was God's covenant with one man, Abraham,[2] and his descendants. The third was the covenant with the Israelites after God had brought them out from slavery in Egypt.[3] God promised them protection and blessing provded they kept his commandments. In Judaism and Christianity these commandments have been seen as the cornerstone of morality and their influence of subsequent European and world culture cannot be over-estimated. The full list of the commandments is:

1 You shall have no other gods before me.

2 You shall not make for yourself a graven image, or any likeness of anything that is in heaven above, or that is in the earth beneath, or that is in the water under the earth; you shall not bow down to them

[1] Genesis 9.
[2] Genesis 15.
[3] Exodus 19.

11

or serve them; for I the Lord your God am a jealous God, visiting the iniquity of the fathers upon the children to the third and fourth generation of those who hate me ...

3 You shall not take the name of the Lord your God in vain ...

4 Remember the sabbath day, to keep it holy. Six days shall you labour and do all your work; but the seventh is a sabbath to the Lord your God; in it you shall not do any work, you, or your son, or your daughter, your manservant, or your maidservant, or your cattle, or the sojourner who is within your gates; for in six days the Lord made heaven and earth, the sea and all that is in them, and rested the seventh day; therefore the Lord blessed the sabbath day and hallowed it.

5 Honour your father and mother, that your days may be long in the land which the Lord your God gives you.

6 You shall not kill.

7 You shall not commit adultery.

8 You shall not steal.

9 You shall not bear false witness against your neighbour.

10 You shall not covet your neighbour's house; you shall not covet your neighbour's wife, or his manservant, or his maidservant, or his ox, or his ass, or anything that is your neighbour's. (Exodus: 20:3–17)

These commandments –'The Decalogue' as they have been termed – have been the foundation of Jewish, Christian and Islamic morality and religious attitudes to sex. Any discussion of sexuality must take them seriously. The first point to note is that there is only one specific and one non-specific reference to sexuality. The seventh commandment prohibits adultery and the tenth prohibits a man coveting his neighbour's wife.

These commandments have great depth and power but they, like the rest of the Bible, are culturally conditioned. This sounds simple, but it is enormously important. If these commandments, and other commandments of God, are literally considered to be divinely dictated by God and to be obeyed to the letter, then huge problems arise. For instance:

- Nothing in these commandments prohibits sex before marriage, sex foreplay, contraception, masturbation, homosexuality (whether male or female) or, indeed, a vast range of other actions which some would today regard as wrong, such as insider share dealing, pollution of the environment, torture, hard core pornography, etc.
- The second commandment expressly forbids any representation of any animal, bird, fish or plant – yet such pictures are readily accepted in Western society. In Islam, this prohibition is taken literally. If one goes into any mosque one will never find a picture, instead there are incredibly beautiful patterns – patterns do not contravene the second commandment. In Western society we have come to recognize that this commandment is not to be taken at face value, it is tied in with a prohibition against worshipping idols. Once this is understood, we can see that having pictures and sculptures does not offend the underlying principle of the commandment. The same approach may be taken with the commandments about adultery and covetousness.
- The fourth commandment expressly forbids any work to be done on the sabbath. Yet this commandment is not just routinely ignored in Western society, it is not even strictly applied by Christians. Orthodox Jews do take it with great seriousness, but no Christian would accept the sort of strict interpretation to this command given by the ancient Rabbis and still applied today in Orthodox Judaism. Indeed, Jesus himself, as we shall see in chapter 4, is recorded as rejecting this interpretation, saying that by taking the command literally people had missed its point.
- The sixth commandment expressly forbids any killing. Some early Christians took this seriously and also took seriously Jesus' commands never to take revenge, to turn the other cheek, etc.

However, from the time of St Augustine onwards it was accepted by the Christian Church that killing in a just war was not just morally acceptable but was a positive moral duty. The right to kill in self-defence was also accepted and some Christians today support capital punishment.

- The tenth commandment lists a wife as just one more possession along with other possessions of the neighbour. It is as wrong to covet the neighbour's wife as it is to covet his ox, his male servant or his ass. We could extend this today to his car, his house or his job. The point is that this commandment is to do with a prohibition against jealousy or wishing to own things that belong to someone else. Today, when wives are not regarded, by most people, as possessions, this commandment does not apply in the sense it orginally had.

- The tenth commandment is entirely expressed in male terms. There is a prohibition against a man coveting a neighbour's wife, but nothing against a woman coveting a neighbour's husband. The cultural bias is clear – today we recognize this and say, 'Of course, the commandment applies to both men and women,' but in saying this we are already going beyond the text. We are interpreting.

The Decalogue is only a part of the commands meant to have been laid down by God. In the same and the following chapter as that in which the Ten Commandments are recorded, it goes on to say:

And the Lord said to Moses: 'Thus you shall say to the people of Israel' …you shall not make gods of gold or silver to be with me, nor shall you make for yourselves gods of gold … When you buy a Hebrew slave, he shall serve six years, and in the seventh he shall go free. If he comes in single, he shall go out single; if he comes in married, then his wife shall go out with him … When a man sells his daughter as a slave she shall not go out as the male slaves do. If she does not please her master, who has designated her for himself, then he shall let her be redeemed; he shall have

14

no right to sell her to a foreign people ... If he designates her for his son, he shall deal with her as with a daughter. If he takes another wife for himself, he shall not diminish her food or clothing, or her marital rights.[4]

Those who wish the Ten Commandments to be taken literally as direct commandments by God would also have to accept that God is here approving arrangements for slavery, for selling daughters into slavery, for multiple marriages, etc. Few would be willing to claim this. Chapters 21 to 23 continue with a long list of commands by God, such as:

a) If a man sleeps with an unmarried woman, he must marry her and pay her father the bride price (Exodus 22:16).
b) All sorceresses must be killed (Exodus 22:18).
c) Anyone having sex with an animal shall be killed (Exodus 22:19).
d) Crops may only be planted; vineyards only harvested and olives only taken from olive groves for seven years – in the seventh year no crops may be planted so that the poor can collect any produce (Exodus 23:10–11).

No one would consider that these rules apply today. It needs to be accepted that the Ten Commandments, like so much else in the Bible, contain great wisdom but need to be understood in the context and time in which they were written. From within the text, there is no essential difference between the command not to commit adultery and the command not to make images of animals or birds; not to work on the sabbath or not to kill. ALL require interpretation and none can be taken at face value.

The Decalogue provided the foundation stone for subsequent theological reflection on questions of morality. However, little emphasis was placed on sexuality – many other areas had a higher

[4] Exodus 20:22–23; 21:2,3,7–10, repeated in Deuteronomy 5:11–22.

priority. Nevertheless, by looking at particular passages dealing with sexual matters in the Bible, clear indications can be obtained of the practices that were considered unacceptable. In the text, God is recorded as directly commanding the following:

1 Any male whose testicles are crushed or whose penis is cut off cannot be numbered amongst God's elect (Deuteronomy 23:1).

2 If any man has a 'wet dream' so that he has an issue of sperm in the night, then he shall be regarded as unclean and in need of purification (Deuteronomy 23:10).

3 Prostitution as part of the Canaanite religious cult is forbidden by God.[5] (Not all prostitution was forbidden – for instance Tamar offered herself to Judah and this was accepted as was Rahab's prostitution.)[6]

4 If a woman had a child, she was unclean (because of the blood involved) and could not take part in any religious activities until she had been purified by the priest. After the birth of a son, the period of impurity was 40 days whilst after the birth of a daughter it was 80 days.[7] It is significant that, until 1980, the Church of England's Prayer Book contained a service for 'Thanksgiving of women after childbirth' – the origin of this was a similar service entitled 'The purification of women after childbirth'. Women were considered impure as a result of the birth process and this resulted from the command in the Hebrew scriptures.

These appear to be cultural taboos attributed to God by the writers of the ancient records, but there may well be a difference between these attributions and what was directly commanded by God. They

---

[5] Deuteronomy 23:17.
[6] For the story of Tamar and Judah see Genesis 38:1–10. The role of Rahab in assisting the Israelites to enter Jericho (recorded in chapters 2 to 6 of Joshua) is dealt with in chapter 3 of this book.
[7] Leviticus 12:2–5.

were based on keeping Israel pure (hence deformed people or those with infectious diseases were to be excluded) and on the idea of cultic purity which meant that any bodily emissions from sexual organs were considered to be defiling. We have here a primitive understanding of bodily processes and may therefore conclude that such commandments have little to teach us today. The question arises, of course, why teachings about sexual behaviour should be any the less culturally conditioned, and it is with this question that this book is partly concerned.

THREE

Women and Sex
in the Old Testament

Following the creation stories in Genesis, the Hebrew Scriptures record a number of approaches to the relation between men and women. These can be broadly differentiated as follows:

a) The Patriarchal period extending from Abraham through to Moses and the exodus from Egypt. According to the text, this was a period of wandering, nomadic families moving with their large herds over wide areas.

b) The period of the Judges and the Kings when there were independent kingdoms roughly within the area of the modern Israel. The kingdoms were united under Saul, David and Solomon. The divided kingdoms of Israel and Judah continued to be ruled by kings until the destruction of Jerusalem by the Babylonians.

c) The exilic and post-exilic period from the time of the Israelites being taken away to slavery in Babylon, their eventual return and the rebuilding of Jerusalem up to the time of Jesus.

These will be dealt with separately.

a) The Patriarchal Period

This is the period of the great patriarchs or 'Fathers' of Israel extending up to the time of the exile into Egypt. The key figures are Noah, Abraham, Jacob and Joseph. In this society, marriage normally represented the son of one family acquiring the daughter of another – it involved a contractual relationship and was normally negotiated by the two families. The acquisition was a form of 'purchase' – a marriage gift, sometimes described as a 'bride-price', was given by the husband-to-be to his fiancée's father.[1] However, this is not straightforward. The wife did not simply become the property of her husband or of his family. For instance, if the husband died, the widow had the right to remain in his family by marrying another member of it, or she could return to her own family unit. The 'bride-price' was not the money paid as if for the purchase of goods   it may have been seen as compensation to the daughter's family for their loss or, on some accounts, the money may even have been the property of the bride to-be. For instance, in Genesis 31, Rachel and Leah, the two wives of Jacob, say that their father had 'been using up the money given for us' – the implication being that the bride price was not their father's to spend.

The husband acquired firm rights over the wife, but these rights were not total – the wife also had rights. In particular, she had the right to food, clothing and the right to sleep with her husband.[2] Such rights, were, therefore fairly minimal. For instance when Abraham went down to Egypt, he knew that Sarah was very beautiful and was nervous that someone might kill him in order to sleep with her. He therefore told Sarah to pretend to be his sister.[3] Reports of Sarah's beauty were sent to the King of Egypt (the Pharaoh) who, thinking she was single, married her and gave great riches to Abraham. However, God punished Pharaoh (seemingly unfairly as he believed Sarah to be unmarried) and Pharaoh then discovered she was married. He therefore sent Abraham and his wife away. Abraham played the same trick again later when he met with King Abimelech, who then took Sarah but before he could make love to her God stopped him, threatening him with death. Abimelech, naturally enough, was rather upset as he did not know that he had done anything wrong.[4]

[1] Cf. Genesis 34:12, Exodus 22:16–17 and 1 Samuel 18:25.
[2] Exodus 21:10.
[3] Genesis 12:10–16.
[4] Genesis 20:1–7.

The wife was expected to produce children and, if she did not, the fault was considered always to be with the woman – never with the man. Lack of children was a source of shame to the woman and children were the greatest possible blessing. They were seen as a gift of God. A wife without children might consider her life not worth living – for instance, Rachel says to Jacob 'Give me children, or I shall die!'[5] Children were particularly vital as there was no idea of life after death, and men considered that they lived on through their children – so without children their 'name' could not live on.

A childless woman, however, had a remedy – she could give her slave girl to her husband who could then bear children for her. For instance, Jacob's wife, Leah, had four sons. Jacob's second wife, Rachel, did not have children and was jealous of Leah, so she told Jacob to sleep with her slave girl, Bilhah. Having done so, Bilhah had a son to whom she gave birth 'between the knees' of Rachel and it thus became Rachel's son for which she rejoiced and thanked God.[6] Rachel did the same again, sending her husband to sleep with Bilhah and thereby getting another son.

A very similar situation occurred when Abraham's wife, Sarah, could not have children. Sarah sent Abraham to sleep with her slave girl, Hagar, and then gave her to Abraham as his wife.[7] The child whom she had, named Ishmael, was Abraham's first born but, when Sarah herself had a son later, Abraham drove Ishmael out into the desert at her request. Sarah said to Abraham:

'Cast out this slave woman with her son; for the son of this slave woman shall not be heir with my son Isaac.'[8]

Hagar and Ishmael were cast out into the desert and would have died had God not taken pity on them and allowed them to survive. (Ishmael, interestingly, is seen as one of the key figures in Islam –

[5] Genesis 30:1.
[6] Genesis 30:3–6.
[7] Genesis 16:1–15.
[8] Genesis 21:10.

guarded by God and making his home in the wildness of the desert areas, the forerunner of the wandering desert nomads of Arabia.)

There is one recorded case of a man not having any sons giving his daughter to a slave in order that the daughter could bear a son for him.[9] Because the father of the child was the man's slave, the child could become his son rather than his grandson.

The number of families in the Patriarchal period was fairly small although they would have been extended, with many members. Marriages of cousins to each other was allowed and marriage to a half-sister is described without any sense that this was wrong.[10] Later, however, sex between a half-brother and a half-sister was condemned.[11]

b) The Period of the Judges and the Kings

Jacob and his sons went down into Egypt with their families due to a drought in Palestine, and grew into a large company of people. They were initially allowed to work as free people thanks to the influence of Joseph who became one of the Pharaoh's chief counsellors, but in later years they became slaves to the Egyptians, exiles who worked at building and other tasks, but maintaining their own identity and above all their worship of God. Eventually, Moses and Aaron led an exodus out from Egypt, across the Red Sea and into the Sinai desert where, for many years, they lived in the desert in conditions almost harsher than those from which they had escaped. The text records that it was in this period that the Ten Commandments were given.

In terms of marriage, after the people of Israel came into the land of Canaan, women were treated very much as a possession. Women were not simply the property of their husbands – they had some rights, but these were restricted. It is significant, for instance, that only men could divorce or 'disown' women because only men had

[9] 1 Chronicles 2:34–41.
[10] For instance in Genesis 20:12 and later in 2 Samuel 13:13.
[11] Ezekiel 22:11.

effective ownership rights; the wife had no freedom to dispose of herself.[12]

The following stories are indicative of the mind-set of the times, which clearly varied over the years:

Rahab

After Moses died, Joshua led the people of Israel down into the land God had promised them, but this land was already populated and it was well defended. The Israelites, therefore, had to conquer the land and, in particular, had to destroy the city of Jericho. Joshua sent two spies into Jericho before his attack. These two men came to the city and went and lodged with a Canaanite prostitute called Rahab. However, the authorities discovered their presence and sent troops to search for them. Rahab hid them on the roof of her house and after the troops had left spoke to them. She said that everyone in the city was afraid because of Joshua's huge army and knew that God had released the Israelites from slavery under the Egyptians and had helped them to defeat other enemies. She said she would hide them and would release them provided they promised that when Joshua attacked her city she and her father's family would not be harmed. This they agreed to, and said that she was to mark the window of her house with red wool. They then returned to Joshua, hiding from Jericho's troops who were searching for them.

After the successful attack by Joshua's troops, Joshua killed every man, woman and child and all the animals in the city except for Rahab and her family, who lived with the Israelites for the remainder of their lives.

The significant part of this story for the purpose of this book is that Rahab was a prostitute who was nevertheless the key to Israel's successful attack and not once is there any mention of disapproval of her profession. What is at issue in this story is 'who is on the Lord's side' – in other words, who serves God and who opposed God. Only Rahab, out of the whole of Jericho, is portrayed as helping

---

[12] Deuteronomy 24:1–4.

God's elect forces and so only she is saved. There is no question of her being virtuous or particularly worthy – the only issue is that she sided with God's forces against her own people.

Samson

Samson was a young boy who was blessed by God. Samson fell in love with a young Philistine woman and married her. However, he told a riddle to thirty of her companions and placed a bet that they could not get the answer. The companions took the bet but failed to get the answer, so they persuaded Samson's new wife to find the answer and to tell them – she felt a natural loyalty to her country folk and passed on his secret. When they were able to answer the riddle, Samson was furious and rejected her, so her father gave her to Samson's best man. Later, Samson changed his mind and went back to her father's house to collect her. The father told Samson that he had given her away and offered the younger daughter as a substitute. Samson again lost his temper and went and burned the fields (using foxes with torches in their tails) of the father's friends. When the friends found out, they came and killed the father and his daughter. Samson then went and slaughtered the father's killers.[13]

In the years that followed, Samson had sex with a prostitute and his enemies lay in wait outside for him, but Samson got up at midnight and pulled up the gates of the city and carried them up a neighbouring hill.[14] The next woman Samson took was Delilah, another Philistine (in later centuries it was to become a crime against God to marry a non-Jew, yet at this time it is seen as a feature of Samson's strength). Delilah was persuaded by Samson's enemies to finally get the better of him. She wheedled the secret of his strength out of him, again out of loyalty to her country folk whom Samson had treated so badly. Thus his enemies were able to kill him, but not before his strength returned one last time and he was able to

[13] Judges 14:1–15:8.
[14] Judges 16:1–3.

bring down the house in which he and his enemies were and was thus able to kill them all.[15]

Samson is generally regarded as a man in the service of God, yet it is clear he made love to various attractive young women who were not from his own people, was often betrayed and none of this was considered to be morally unacceptable. Only when his hair was cut off did God desert him by taking away his powers because his parents had been told by an angel before Samson's birth that this should not happen.[16]

The Old Man from Ephraim[17]

There were twelve tribes in Israel, supposedly descended from the twelve sons of Jacob and each lived in a certain area. A Levite traveller and his servant came to a town in the territory of the tribe of Benjamin where a man from the tribe of Ephraim was staying. They needed somewhere to spend the night and no one would take them in. They sat in the square of the town until the old man from Ephraim saw him and invited them into his house.

The Levite and his servant washed and they were eating and drinking when various crude men from the town came beating on the door demanding to have sex with the visitor – in other words we have here an example of the wish to homosexually rape the visitor. The old man told them that they should not do this wicked thing but instead offered to them his daughter and the Levite's concubine, saying to them:

'Behold, here are my virgin daughter and my concubine; let me bring them out now. Ravish them and do with them what seems good to you; but against this man do not do so vile a thing.'

The men would not listen, so the old man seized the concubine (a concubine was not quite a wife, but enjoyed a significant status in a

[15] Judges 16:4–30.
[16] Judges 13:5.
[17] Judges 19:1–21:24.

man's house) and pushed her outside. The men raped her and 'abused her all night long until morning'. At daybreak they let her go. As morning came, the woman staggered back to the old man's house and fell at his door. When the Levite opened the door the concubine was lying on the threshold with her hands on the door. The Levite told her to get up and come with him to his home in Ephraim but there was no reply. When he got her home, he cut her up into twelve pieces and sent the pieces throughout all the tribes of Israel asking for vengeance.

The eleven tribes of Israel gathered and vowed vengeance against the tribe of Benjamin whose members had behaved so badly. The vengeance took place after a great battle when most of the men, women and cattle of the tribe of Benjamin were destroyed. After taking this vengeance, the other tribes of Israel decided that Benjamin had been punished enough and it was now necessary to build up the tribe again. There were some men of the tribe left, but not many, and no women. All the eleven tribes of Israel had sworn not to give any woman in marriage to Benjamin's men. The tribes of Israel agreed, therefore, that the remaining Benjamin men could go to Shiloh and abduct enough women from there to restart their tribe and they would make it right with the Shiloh men.

We have here a story of sexual abuse and rape of the worst kind – but the significant points are not the woman's position but the abuse of strangers and the violation of the property of the old man. The points being made are that the stranger is sacred and must not be harmed. The Levite's rights and the law of hospitality had been infringed and the man from Ephraim demanded vengeance. The vengeance was taken on the whole tribe of Benjamin and women were obtained, like a commodity, to repopulate the tribe after its near destruction. This type of story gives an indication of the cultural *milieu* in which the Bible stories and understanding of God developed – the cultural distance separating us from that time is immense and this must be taken into account when considering the relevance of any biblical text for today.

Ruth

Naomi was the widow of a man who came from Bethlehem. She had two sons who took wives from among the Moabite people amongst whom they were living. The two sons died, leaving the widow and two step-daughters. The widow, Naomi, told the step-daughters to return to their own people as she could not provide husbands for them as she had no other children. One did so but the other, Ruth, swore not to be parted from Naomi either in life or death and returned with Naomi to her own country. The two widows returned, therefore, to Bethlehem in considerable poverty and they gleaned behind those who collected corn. The practice of 'gleaning' was laid down in Israelite tradition – women were allowed to follow behind the reapers and to pick up the ears of corn that had dropped. One older man, Boaz, noticed Ruth and allowed her to glean in his field. He told his young men not to molest her and arranged for them to drop ears of corn that she could pick up. Rejoicing, Ruth went back to Naomi, who told her that she must go and see where Boaz was sleeping and then go and 'uncover his blanket'. The actual verse in the RSV Bible is as follows:

> And when Boaz had eaten and drunk, and his heart was merry, he went to lie down at the end of the heap of grain. And she came softly and uncovered his feet, and lay down.[18]

Boaz woke and asked who was there. Ruth asked him to spread his blanket over her which was a gesture of proposal of marriage. He praised her because she had come to him rather than to a younger man – the text is not clear as to whether they made love that night (the reference to Boaz's feet is almost certainly a euphemism for more intimate parts of his body – the same euphemism is used elsewhere), although it is perhaps likely particularly given Boaz's reference to Ruth having come to him rather than to a younger man. Boaz was a close but not the nearest relative and first had to

[18] Ruth 3:7.

negotiate with the closest relative to ensure he had the right to take her as his wife. He then bought her with some land – the two came together as a package. Boaz and Ruth duly married and were to become the great grandparents of Israel's greatest man, King David.

Ruth showed great loyalty to and love for her mother-in-law as well as great courage – she also trusted the God of her husband's family against all rational assessment. With her mother-in-law's advice, she showed initiative in securing a wealthy husband who would safeguard her and Naomi. Her tactics might fairly be described as seduction, but the tactics succeeded and Ruth and Naomi's prosperity was secured. Such blatant advances to Boaz were considered resourceful and praiseworthy, and Ruth is held out as one of the great heroines of the Bible.

David and Bathsheba[19]
King David was looking down from his palace roof and saw a beautiful woman, Bathsheba, bathing. She had just had a period and was bathing to clean herself – this had both a practical and a ritual purpose. Cleanliness in the heat of Israel was always regarded as important, but it was the ritual cleansing from impurity that was more religiously significant. David sent messengers to her, had her brought to him and made love to her.

Bathsheba returned home and later discovered she was pregnant. Bathsheba's husband, Uriah, was away on campaign and David sent a message to the army commander to have Uriah sent to him at the palace. When Uriah arrived David asked him how the war was going and then dismissed him, telling him to go back to his house and wash. David expected Uriah to go home and make love to his wife – then her pregnancy could be thought to be due to Uriah. However, Uriah refused to return home while his fellow soldiers continued on campaign and stayed with other soldiers at David's palace. David then got him drunk hoping that he would then go

[19] 2 Samuel 11:2–12:25.

home to sleep with his wife, but this did not work either and Uriah refused to return home.

So David sent Uriah back to the army commander with a message which said:

> 'Set Uriah in the forefront of the hardest fighting, and then draw back from him that he may be struck down, and die.'[20]

The plan worked, and Uriah was duly killed. Bathsheba lamented him for the required time and then David sent for her and she became another of his wives. We now see, however, a developing sense of what is and what is not acceptable. The prophet Nathan is sent by God to David and tells him the following story:

> 'There were two men in a certain city, the one rich and the other poor. The rich man had very many flocks and herds, but the poor man had nothing but one little ewe lamb, which he had bought. And he brought it up, and it grew up with him and with his children; it used to eat of his morsel and drink from his cup, and lie in his bosom, and it was like a daughter to him. Now there came a traveller to the rich man, and he was unwilling to take one of his own flock or herd to prepare for the wayfarer who had come to him, but he took the poor man's lamb, and prepared it for the man who had come to him.'[21]

When David was told this story he was furious and said that whoever had done this deserved to die because he showed no pity and decreed that the man should restore the lamb fourfold. Nathan then said: 'You are the man.'

Nathan then prophesied that because of what David had done 'the sword would never depart from his house'. David had dealt secretly and Nathan prophesied that he would be punished publicly. David repented and asked forgiveness and Nathan said that his life

[20] 2 Samuel 11:15.
[21] 2 Samuel 12:1–4.

would be spared but the baby born to Bathsheba would die. The child duly fell sick and David prayed to God and fasted for the child's life, but he still died. Immediately, David stopped weeping and went in to make love to Bathsheba again. She became pregnant and her son became the great King Solomon – the wisest and richest of all the kings of Israel.

This story is important as there is an increasing understanding that certain conduct is unacceptable and will be punished by God – even though it is done in secret. Yet, while the death of the son is David's punishment, his next son by Bathsheba becomes a great king and a real joy to David. Thus, in a way, David's sin produced excellent results for him, although the dissension and violence within his own household do indeed ensue.

The prophet Nathan's criticism is not prompted by David's sexual activity – but by his theft of the property of someone who was poor. Again, therefore, we have the situation where a woman is looked on as a man's property and punishment comes if she is stolen away. William Countryman expresses the point like this:

> If an outsider did have sexual intercourse with a married woman this constituted a theft of her husband's right to legitimate offspring. Like any loss of property to anyone, this also shamed the husband and reduced the family's status in the community.[22]

David's son, Solomon, became king and was held to be the wealthiest and the wisest of all the kings of the area – indeed the phrase 'the wisdom of Solomon' is widely used even today. However, Solomon made love to many women. He was reputed to have had seven hundred wives and three hundred concubines. The problem raised by God's prophets was not the number of women he had, but that many of them were foreigners – he made love to a daughter of the Egyptian Pharaoh and to Moabite, Ammonite, Edomite, Sioanian and Hittite women.[23] There is no mention at all of this being in any

[22] L. William Countryman, *Dirt, Greed and Sex*, SCM, 1989, p. 157.
[23] 1 Kings 11:1.

sense morally unacceptable – he was punished by God, through his successors, because he had been seduced by these foreign women into worshipping other gods and because he built altars to the gods of his women.

c) The Exile and the Post-Exilic Period

In due course, the kingdom of Israel was overthrown. The Babylonians defeated the army of Israel, the walls of Jerusalem were razed to the ground, the Temple destroyed and most of the inhabitants carried off in slavery to Babylon. The people of Israel were now in a second exile. The first exile had occurred in Egypt and Moses and Aaron had led the Israelites from there to Canaan which had been the scene of so much of their history. Now, once again, they were exiled – this time in Babylon.

Throughout the long years of exile, the people of Israel are recorded as keeping their faith in the God they believed had destroyed their city but who had promised it would be rebuilt. Out of this period of exile came various significant stories, and none more so than the story of Esther.

Esther

Esther was a Jew, one of the wives of King Ahasuerus of Persia in whose empire the Jews were held captive. Her adoptive father, Mordecai, learned of a plot by one of the king's chief ministers, Haman, to kill all the Jews (rather similar to the modern holocaust) and the only hope was to change the mind of the king. Mordecai himself had no access to the King, and Esther, at great risk to her own life, used her feminine wiles to persuade the king to a dinner with Haman. There she pleaded for the lives of all her people, knowing full well that a refusal by the king meant the end of her own life as well as the lives of all the Jews in the empire. Her persuasive tactics succeeded and the Jews were saved. To this day, Jews celebrate the festival of Purim which runs over two days and is a time for the exchange of gifts and for rejoicing because of their deliverance from a time of despair.

The importance of this story is that, even in their darkest hour, the Jewish nation will be safeguarded, yet the heroine of this story is woman, one of a large number of wives of a foreign king. Because of her position, Esther would have had no status within Judaism – yet this woman was the cause of salvation for the whole Jewish nation.

Stories such as that of Ruth and Esther stress the strength and resolve of women and helped to redress the balance of the biblical narrative which would otherwise have tended to cast women in a limited, subservient role. There are also passages which praise women's roles as homemakers and mothers. These roles are shown as demanding great resources, for example, in Proverbs 31:

> She considers a field and buys it; with the fruit of her hands she plants a vineyard. She perceives that her merchandise is profitable. She opens her arms to the poor and reaches her hands to the needy. Strength and dignity are her clothing. She opens her mouth with wisdom and the teaching of kindness is on her tongue.

This positive view of women in the home does not, however, undermine the essentially subservient place of women in the sexual sphere and the general lack of rights of females.

By the end of the Old Testament period, Jewish thinkers had transformed the rules regarding purity into rules regarding sexual misconduct. The Hebrew Scriptures were, according to a legendary story, translated into Greek from the original Hebrew by 70 scholars (hence this new translation was called the Septuagint – from the Greek for seventy). In this translation, although not in the original Hebrew nor indeed in one of the versions of the Septuagint, adultery is raised into the leading place in the list of sins above theft and murder.[24] We see here, therefore, the clear wish of Jewish rabbis to

---

[24] Exodus 20:13–15 and Deuteronomy 5:17 (Septuagint).

raise the profile of sexual sin so that what was previously impure is now identified with what was morally bad. This was to have very considerable implications for Christian thought in the early years of the Christian Church.

Summary

The attitude to sexual relationships, sexual intercourse, child-bearing and the like in the Hebrew Scriptures was down-to-earth and frank. Procreation was, implicitly, the main objective of marriage – there was little idea of an afterlife and children were, therefore, the way in which a man could see himself as surviving his own death. There was a developing sense of understanding of how human beings should relate to each other and many of the rules laid down had to do with Jewish attitudes to property and purity. These purity rules gradually became developed into moral rules governing, in particular, the sexual arena. Understanding how the people of Israel wrestled with these problems is important, but one cannot decide what the correct reaction should be to sexual issues at the dawning of the new millennium merely by referring to the understanding prevailing in ancient Israel.

FOUR

Jesus: A Scandalous Figure

It must be recognized at the outset that determining what Jesus actually said, as opposed to what the gospel writers say that he said, is almost impossible. An earlier title in this series, *The Puzzle of the Gospels*,[1] explores such issues in detail, making it clear that one cannot simply read the gospel stories and assume that these are accurate records of Jesus' words. There are a variety of traditions recorded in the gospels – some of them contradictory – and no certainty. Having said that, the gospel stories lie at the heart of the Christian tradition and have had a profound influence.

Family Life

In the Hebraic tradition at the time of Jesus, family life was still patriarchal. The biblical passages examined in chapter 3 have provided clear evidence of a culture in which wives and children were essentially seen as property. Sexual activity was aimed at procreation and women were meant to keep themselves virginal until their 'ownership' had passed from their fathers to their husband (cf. p. 19). Married women had to be faithful to their husbands, as only by so doing could the legitimate offspring of the father be guaranteed – adultery represented the theft of the property of the man. The man had full rights over his wife's body and full access to her for sexual purposes. Women were intended for one end – marriage – and from an early age the preoccupation of parents was to ensure a successful marriage for their daughters.

[1] Peter Vardy & Mary Mills, *The Puzzle of the Gospels*, Fount Paperbacks, 1995.

Once married, the women of a household were respected and became an important part of society – outside of marriage, however, they had no status or identity at all. Prostitutes were a threat to the established order of society and to family life – they were outcasts. Widows were treated with respect and were given charity but had little status. Women could take no part in religious life in their own right and religious leaders had to be male. The coming of age of a young man was an event of singular importance whereas the crucial rite of passage for a woman was marriage.

It may at first sight seem surprising, but almost all these features of Jewish life at the time of Jesus could be seen to apply to Victorian society or to much of the world endorsed by traditional 'Christian' values. To be sure, there are some exceptions – but these cannot mask the overall similarity. Yet Jesus deliberately and consistently subverted this whole way of looking at family life and the position of women – he was radical, yet his teaching has become overlaid by new layers of convention. A few examples will illustrate this:

1 Jesus was born of a virgin – this sounds an attractive idea to Christians who have been brought up with this phrase, but it in fact means that Mary was an unmarried mother and therefore a social outcast. Yet this is the woman God chose as the mother for Jesus. Also, it was Mary, a woman, rather than Joseph who was recorded as being with Jesus through much of his ministry.

2 According to Mark's gospel (3:21), when Jesus started his teaching, his whole family considered him to be mad and came to him to exert their authority over him. The background to this and the family's right to take this action was clearly established in the Jewish tradition, yet Jesus repudiated them and rejected their claim to authority.

3 Jesus called disciples to leave everything (Luke 5:11) and to follow him – this meant leaving their families behind. When James and John were called from their fishing boat, they were called by Jesus to leave their father to whom they should have owed supreme loyalty.

34

4   When someone who wished to follow Jesus asked first to be given permission to bury his father, Jesus told him to 'Let the dead bury their dead' (Luke 9:60) – thus challenging normal conventions and the very high value given to the burial of a close relative and the family ties this involved.

5   Jesus was at home with the 'outsiders' – those rejected by Jewish family life and Jewish society. This did not just mean the Roman centurion, the tax collector or the Samaritan woman, it also meant that he was at home with the single woman, the prostitute, the woman who had been living with a series of men. He treated them as friends and, whilst on occasion pointing out their failings, in no way indicated that these failings were any greater than those of the supposedly holy and pious who were convinced of their own self-righteousness. Indeed his real anger and condemnation were reserved for the latter.

6   When Jesus was surrounded by a crowd and children tried to run to him, his disciples pushed them away. But Jesus told them to let the children through to him, as people in his kingdom would be like them. He also said that the person who wanted to follow him had to become like a little child (Luke 18:17). These are such well-worn phrases that it is easy to forget their impact – a child had no status at all in the traditional family. Only when he (and the male pronoun is used deliberately here) became an adult did he become an individual, and even then was subservient to his father – yet Jesus says that the child is the greatest in his kingdom.

7   Jesus is quoted by the gospels as saying that his followers had to 'hate' their families. Modern commentators sometimes translate the Greek word as 'like less', but this is inaccurate – the textual evidence is clear and the correct translation is, indeed, 'hate'. Such so-called 'hard' sayings of Jesus tend to be ignored by modern commentators who wish to sanitize Jesus' message but this is to misinterpret him. What he said was in accordance with the rest of his teaching – anyone placing family at the centre of their lives cannot place God in this position.

8 The status of women in the Old Testament clearly depended on their relationship to their own family or the family of their husband. As described in the case of Ruth (cf. pp. 26–27), a widow had no one to turn to except for one of these family groups. If she could not obtain help here, her position could be desperate. Yet when Jesus was on the cross, he commends his mother to his friend, John, and he commends John to her. From then on their relationship should be as a son to a mother – undermining the traditional family ties and making clear that, in Jesus' new kingdom, family relationships were not decisive.

Jesus' message challenged traditional understanding of some Hebraic teaching. A human being's identity was no longer to be found as a member of the family or national group – instead each human being had to exist as an individual before God and everything had to be put in second place to this, even family ties. This marked the major distinction between Jesus' teaching and much of the Hebrew Scriptures, and shows a significant change in the understanding of human relationship and responsibility. This insight lies behind the emphasis in the Christian tradition on celibacy. It has been held that the celibate way of life enables those who opt for it to single-mindedly devote themselves to centring their lives on God and living lives of radical, non-preferential love for others. Family life, it has been held, can make this more difficult. Sadly, today, this highly positive view of celibacy is often overlaid by stress on the negative side which emphasizes, as one of the main factors, renunciation of all sexual activity.

Jesus' Comments in the Sexual Arena

Considering the attention given by Christians in subsequent generations to matters sexual, Jesus himself had remarkably little to say on the subject. As the Anglican theologian Joseph Fletcher observed:

Jesus said nothing about birth control, large or small families, childlessness, homosexuality, masturbation, fornication, pre-marital intercourse, sterilization, artificial insemination, abortion, sex foreplay, petting and courtship.[2]

However, there are references in the gospels to some matters covered in this book and these must clearly be taken seriously. In particular, Jesus is recorded as referring to divorce and adultery and to a woman who had been living with a series of men to whom she was not married. These comments will need to be considered separately under the specific chapter headings which are to follow.

Leslie Houlden, in *Ethical Decisions and the New Testament*, maintains that the gospel stories were written down some time after Jesus' death by his disciples and that it is almost impossible to arrive at the actual words he said. Instead, he argues, we should ask:

What is the teaching of Jesus likely to have been to lead to the attitudes which we know from the New Testament to have prevailed in the early Church?[3]

Houlden maintains, as does Anthony Harvey in *Strenuous Commands*, that Jesus' teaching is to be seen as a series of challenges to the individual to model his or her life on the will of God. Jesus did not lay down a series of instructions but instead called his followers to live as members of God's kingdom, showing compassion, understanding, gentleness and forgiveness not just to each other but to everyone. Gareth Moore argues that when Jesus says that a man should not set his heart on another man's wife, he is not laying down a sexual rule – he is warning against the injustice of contravening an important social relationship (the marriage bond) by the man wanting to possess something that does not belong to

[2] Joseph Fletcher, *Situation Ethics*, SCM Press, 1966, p. 139.
[3] Leslie Houlden, *Ethical Decisions and the New Testament*, Christian Theology Trust, 1992.

him. Jesus' motive is, therefore, to stop people being unjust to each other.[4]

Anthony Harvey compares Jesus' approach to that of the Pharisees and Essenes, both of whom laid down rules for people to follow. Jesus, by contrast, called his followers to reflect through their lives God's love for all human beings and to live justly with each other. The teachings of Jesus therefore challenged everyone in a radical way, but it cannot be claimed that he gave clear answers in the sexual arena nor that he considered the sexual arena to be of great significance.

Marriage and Divorce

The Hebrew Scriptures recognize the right of a man to divorce his wife, but no such right is recognized in reverse. However, divorce by the male is possible in most but not all circumstances. If a man rapes a young woman and is then forced to pay her father the bride price and to marry her, he may never then divorce her.[5] Divorce is also forbidden if a man falsely accuses his new wife of not being a virgin. If her father can produce the stained bedclothes showing the evidence that her hymen was broken on the wedding night, then the husband is whipped and may never divorce this wife.

The method of divorce appears straightforward:

> When a man takes a wife and marries her, if then she finds no favour in his eyes because he has found some indecency in her, and he writes her a bill of divorce and puts it in her hand and sends her out of his house, and she departs out of his house ...[6]

This view was not seriously challenged until the time of Jesus although there were debates as to the circumstances which would

[4] Gareth Moore, *Body in Context: Sex in Catholic Thought*, SCM Press, 1992, p. 17.
[5] Deuteronomy 22:29.
[6] Deuteronomy 24:1.

allow a man to divorce his wife. In Matthew 19, the Pharisees ask Jesus whether a man is permitted to divorce his wife for any reason at all. There is an underlying reason for this question, as Pharisees and Sadducees differed in their views and whatever Jesus said he was apparently going to upset someone. The Torah (the Law of Moses) has no detailed teaching on divorce, although it was permitted if the man found in his wife 'something improper'.[7] The Pharisees' question is, of course, framed in the terms one would expect – i.e. regarding male rights to divorce the woman.

Jesus goes back to God's original intention which was for a permanent, indissoluble union between man and woman, and he says that Moses introduced the possibility of divorce simply to take account of human weakness. This was not the ideal. So Jesus is apparently taking a more firm line than the accepted Jewish tradition, although an exception is still allowed:

> I tell you anyone who divorces his wife except for *porneia* and marries another is committing adultery.[8]

The meaning of the Greek word *porneia* is not clear. There are three main alternatives:

a) *Porneia* refers to a woman who was not a virgin when she was married. This has already been discussed above and the basis for the Old Testament allowance of divorce explained. Assuming this is correct, then it is a mistaken translation to regard *porneia* as referring to adultery. The only basis for divorce is the lack of virginal status on marriage, and since this would be discovered on the wedding night, no further possibility for divorce would exist thereafter. Jesus, therefore, removes the concession of adultery as a cause for a man to divorce and effectively forbids it entirely.

---

[7] Deuteronomy 24:1.
[8] Matthew 19:9.

b) *Porneia* refers to adultery. In this case, a man may divorce his wife for her adultery, but not the other way round.

c) Bernard Hoose maintains that *porneia* should be translated as 'fornication'. This meant not simply what is meant by the term today, but also marriage to non-believers. On this basis, Jesus could here be seen to be making a real exception to the general prohibition against divorce and allowing this in the case of a failed marriage to a non-Christian.[9]

Whichever of these alternatives is correct, Jesus can be seen as affirming the role of woman. In the Hebrew Scriptures the man could divorce the wife and she was, therefore, always vulnerable. The wife had, effectively, been the man's property and he could dispose of her provided he had a good reason. This was an entirely one-sided relationship and was not in any sense reciprocal.

The disciples recognized the radical nature of what Jesus said. Their response to his statement on divorce is often not understood because its background is not recognized, but their position is clear:

The disciples said to him, 'If such is the case of a man with his wife, it is not expedient to marry.'[10]

If a woman could no longer be considered as a piece of disposable property, the disciples conclude, then the disadvantages of marriage would outweigh the advantages.

Jesus is recorded as making no statement at all about procreation or about any link between marriage and love. It will not do, therefore, to try to solve dilemmas in the sexual field or about human relationships by appeal to teachings of Jesus. Here, as in so many other areas, Jesus left matters ambiguous, calling his disciples to wrestle with what it means to live in relationship with God in the particular situation in which they find themselves. Jesus brought a

[9] Cf. Bernard Hoose, 'Imitating Jesus and Allowing Divorce', *Priests and People*, September 1987.
[10] Matthew 19:10.

message about God and about salvation, and setting down new rules was not his objective.

It is not possible to be sure what Jesus said at all – whether about marriage or divorce. However, if one attempted (unwisely) to ignore such problems and extract the detailed rules Jesus laid down as recorded in the gospels, then they would be as follows:

- A **woman** goes against God's plan for human beings when she breaks a marriage through *porneia* and thus provokes divorce – even though, in Matthew and Luke, it is the husband who initiates the divorce. The meaning of *porneia* is not clear. In Mark's gospel, provision is also made for the case where the wife deserts the husband.[11]
- A **man** goes against God's plan for creation if he divorces his wife. In the Old Testament, unilateral divorce by the husband is accepted on fairly general grounds. Jesus, however, tightens the rules with his phrase 'But I say to you' and allows divorce only in the case of some unspecified indecency in the wife. A man also rejects God's order of creation if he marries a divorced woman in both the case of
  a) where the woman is divorced because of *porneia*, because he is sanctioning the guilt of the woman, or
  b) if he marries a divorced woman who is innocent, because the man is then accepting the arbitrary action of the husband in divorcing the wife.

Jesus is setting out an ideal and there is no doubt that divorce is a falling short of this ideal – it is not what is intended by God. One cannot, then, divorce or remarry someone who is divorced without acknowledging that there has been a failure which is not in accordance with God's will. Repentance is therefore needed, but in the fallen world in which we live, failure is commonplace, and Jesus also constantly emphasized that mistakes can be and will be forgiven.

[11] Mark 10:12.

One must recognize this ideal for what it is and to try to live up to it, but, where this is not possible, then forgiveness and a new start is always possible.

The Western Christian Church has tended to imply that in the case of divorce and remarriage, forgiveness will not be forthcoming and a new start is not possible. But, as we shall see, this is not in accordance with the teaching of the Eastern Orthodox Church or most Protestant Churches.

Even if it is claimed that Jesus is setting out a new law, the extent to which the recorded saying was culturally bound must be recognized. The summary above shows that the husband can divorce the wife on the grounds of *porneia* but this does not apply the other way round. At the time, this might have been reasonable, but today when the radical equality of Jesus' approach to men and women is recognized, this can be seen to be culturally conditioned.

Jesus said nothing about other sexual matters and, indeed, seemed remarkably disinterested in this area of life compared to others. It is the later Christian Church which elevated the sexual arena to such prominence and this is at variance with Jesus' teaching, although, as we shall see, the Church had good reasons for this emphasis.

Summary

Biblical scholarship shows the great difficulty of determining what Jesus actually said. However, it seems clear that he wished individuals to centre their lives wholly on God and to live lives of radical, non-preferential love for others. The different traditions record Jesus as showing limited concern about sexual behaviour. He appeared to strengthen the traditional Jewish position on divorce by appealing to God's original purpose for creation. It is not clear whether he only permitted divorce on the grounds of adultery, or lack of virginity at the time of marriage, or when the marriage partner was a non-believer. In all areas, he accepted the possibility of human failure and held open the door for forgiveness.

FIVE

Men and Women:
The Early Church Tradition

After Jesus' death his followers reflected on his life and teaching. This period of reflection was long and complex, involving some of the finest minds in the European and Mediterranean world. It was in the centuries that followed Jesus' death that Christian doctrine became established and many of the moral rules were laid down. Trying to understand this development is vital if the nature of present assumptions are to be understood.

Most vital of all were the letters of St Paul, as many of these became included in the Christian biblical canon of the New Testament.

St Paul

We know much of St Paul from the writings of the author of Luke's Gospel and its second volume, the Acts of the Apostles, but we know even more from his own letters. Paul has had a profound influence on the development of Christian ideas on sexuality, but his views are not always consistent. For instance:

- Paul argues that in the Church of Christ there is 'neither male nor female' – all are equal (Galatians 3:28).
- Elsewhere he argues that women must be subject to their husbands (Ephesians 5:22–24) – thus retaining the subservience of women to men found in the Old Testament.

43

Paul compares marriage with the relationship between Christ and the Church.[1] This image, whilst it is positive about marriage, also implies a supremacy of the male over the female just as Christ is the supreme head of the Church – so the Old Testament hierarchical view of marriage is retained here. On the other hand, Paul has a generally negative view of marriage and maintains that Christians should remain unmarried but, if they are too weak to do this, then marriage is permissible.[2]

One reason for this is that Paul believed the end of the world was soon to come. Jesus was expected to return a second time, and Paul anticipated that this would happen sooner rather than later. In this context, marriage was an irrelevance, a distraction from serving God. Jesus himself had said there was no marriage in heaven, and since Jesus was soon expected to establish his heavenly kingdom, marriage was clearly inappropriate. A second and more important reason was that Paul considered that Christian discipleship meant single-mindedly concentrating on the service of God, and marriage, like other worldly pursuits, distracted from this and was thus better avoided. As we shall see, St Augustine was to reject this simplistic teaching.

Paul's views on sexuality are set out in response to problems and differences of interpretation that arose within the Christian Church at Corinth. Some Corinthian Christians maintained that Christians, freed from the old Jewish Law or Torah, could do as they liked in the sexual arena because they had found salvation through faith in Christ and to them everything was permitted. On the other hand, others held that marriage and sexuality of all sorts should be forbidden to Christians. Not surprisingly, these opposed views created dissension within the Church and Paul wrote to deal with these problems.

Modern feminist writers bring a distinctive approach to understanding the New Testament. An important book in this area is Elisabeth Schussler Fiorenza's *In Memory of Her*, in which she argues

[1] Ephesians 5:31–32.
[2] 1 Corinthians 7:7,32–34,38.

44

that the New Testament contains clear evidence of a conflict between a male-dominated view of the young Christian Church and the message of equality Jesus himself preached. Schussler Fiorenza argues that Jesus' original followers were marked by a fundamental equality – a vision of common humanity which abolished the distinction of Jew/Greek, man/woman, free person/ slave. Both Norman Perrin and Reginald Fuller have maintained that it is possible, using the gospels, to reconstruct key elements of the historical message of Jesus and that Jesus' main teachings can be established. For instance:

> A fundamental concern of Jesus was to bring together into a unified group those who responded to his proclamation of the Kingdom of God irrespective of their sex, previous background or history.[3]

Schussler Fiorenza maintains that at the heart of Jesus' message was the preaching of liberation from oppression and, in particular, this message of liberation extended to women who had for so long been oppressed in a male-dominated society. *In Memory of Her* and later books by the same author argue that the institutional Church which took over after Jesus' death sought to reintroduce the lower status of women and St Paul was in the forefront of this move. Schussler Fiorenza sees inconsistencies in the attitude to women. For instance:

> There is neither Jew nor Greek, there is neither slave nor free, there is neither male nor female, for you are all one in Christ Jesus. (Galatians 3:28)

> ... the women should keep silence in the churches. For they are not permitted to speak, but should be subordinate, as even the law says. If there is anything they desire to know, let them ask their husbands at home. For it is shameful for a woman to speak in Church. (1 Corinthians 14:34–36)

[3] Norman Perrin, *New Testament*, 1993, p. 288.

The first can be seen as faithful to Jesus' teaching, whilst the second may be regarded as the result of male prejudice in the young Church. Certainly passages, such as the second of those above, were to have a notable effect on early Church attitudes to gender difference.

Paul's views can be summarized as follows:

1   It is better for a man never to make love to a woman at all and to remain celibate (1 Corinthians 7:1). However, if a person is married when he becomes a Christian, then he should stay as he is (1 Corinthians 7:17–24).

2   Because human beings are weak and are tempted sexually, it is preferable to marry and to release sexual energies within marriage rather than to burn with desire whilst single (1 Corinthians 7:2).

3   Once married, then neither husband or wife has complete control over their own bodies. Neither party should deprive the other of sexual activity unless this is for a short period, for instance to allow time for prayer (1 Corinthians 7:3–7). This passage positively encourages sexual activity within marriage and sexual desire is acknowledged as a fact of life which must not be ignored or rejected.

4   Paul clearly knew of Jesus' teaching about divorce and reinforced it. No Christian should get divorced and, if a woman is separated, then she should either remain as she is or reunite with her husband (1 Corinthians 7:10–11). Paul, with the devout Jewish background that he had, clearly retained the Old Testament idea of the supremacy of the male.

5   In the world in which Paul lived, young people were 'betrothed' by their families at an early age and they would consummate the marriage when they grew up. This raised a problem for young Christians – if they had been engaged by their family, should they make love and consummate the marriage? Paul's view is that it would be better if the man does not make love to his fiancée in order to make her his wife and that the couple should remain chaste,

but, if the man had strong sexual passions, then he would not sin if he made love to her.[4] It should also be noted that Paul considers that only the man makes the decision about sexual activity – the woman's view did not come into the matter.

Paul was himself a celibate but this alone would not explain his preference for a celibate life-style. There is no evidence in the gospels for this position and Paul's view was based on the imminent return of Jesus. Because of this, what mattered was to be ready for this return – all outward states such as marriage were completely unimportant.

Paul is effectively saying: 'Stay as you are whether free or slave, whether circumcised or uncircumcised, whether married or single – none of these outward things matter and anyone who thinks they can find favour with God by changing these outward things misses the point. The only exception is if your sexual desire is so strong that you will fall into sin. In this case marriage will be the lesser evil.'

Plato's Influence

St Paul's views were to have a decisive influence on the development of Christian thought and, particularly, on the idea that the celibate or unmarried state was spiritually superior to the married, and on the view that women were inferior to men. However, it would be mistaken to blame this development entirely on Paul – the early Church was strongly influenced by the Platonic, dualist view of human personhood which held that a person is made up of a spiritual soul or spirit united with matter which makes up the human body. This led to profound scepticism about everything bodily and, therefore, sexual, and to the view that the task of a human being was to subjugate bodily activity to the 'higher' spiritual values. When this Platonic background was combined with St Paul's views, a very negative view of marriage and sexuality emerged.

[4] 1 Corinthians 7:25–28,36–38.

Plato and Aristotle had a great influence on the developing Christian understanding of sexuality although, as we shall see, Aristotle's influence came to the fore much later through the work of St Thomas Aquinas (*c.* 1225–1275) which is discussed in chapter 6. It was Plato who had the greatest influence on the early Church Fathers. Plato considered that love was one of the four ways in which human beings could have access to the Forms – the perfect exemplars of ideas found in this world such as justice, goodness or love. For Plato, this present world was a dance of shadows compared with true, ultimate reality which was timeless and spaceless.

Plato considered that a beautiful soul was contained in a beautiful body – people initially fall in love with the physical appearance of a person, in other words with the body.[5] However, as the love develops each person tends to come to appreciate the inner psyche of the other rather than the outer shell. Each individual is then led beyond this earthly love to seek the perfect Form of Beauty which exists independently of time and space. Physical love is, therefore, but the first stage on a journey and can and should be left behind as one seeks higher, spiritual love. Plato's influence, however, whilst it might have been positive in seeing sexual love as the start of the journey towards God who is love itself, in fact had the opposite influence. Because Plato was a dualist, he played down the physical side of humanity and emphasized the development of the soul.

This was attractive to the early Church Fathers and it led, combined with the influence of St Paul's writings, to the view that chastity was to be preferred to sexual activity and that all sexual activity was to be regarded with suspicion. However, it was Philo of Alexandria who brought Plato's thought together with the Hebraic background and this combination proved a potent influence on the early Church fathers.

[5] In the *Phaedrus* and in the *Symposium*.

Philo of Alexandria

Jews had spread throughout the Mediterranean world by the time of Jesus and there was a large community of Jews in the great Greek city of Alexandria. From here came the highly influential Jewish writer, Philo (*c.* 25 BCE–40 CE). Philo was himself greatly influenced by Plato's thought and brought Judaism and Plato together in a potent combination which had a great impact. We have seen that Plato emphasized the development of the soul and saw the body in largely negative terms. We have also seen in chapter 3 that Jewish thinkers before the time of Jesus had taken the purity rules of the Jewish Pentateuch (the first five books of the Hebrew Scriptures) and transformed them into a negative understanding of sexuality. Philo seized on both these themes.

Philo maintained that the sole purpose of sex was procreation, even within marriage, and he strongly condemned those who had sexual relations during a woman's infertile period or with married women who were known to be sterile. Philo considered women to be objects of pleasure and the instrument of evil — referring back to the story of Adam and Eve. He held that Eve introduced pleasure to the man who would otherwise have been rational. In this sense, Philo maintains that 'woman has been for man the beginning of blameworthy life'.[6]

The Dead Sea Scrolls have revealed a good deal about the Essenes, who practised a strict version of Judaism by means of a flight from the world and its evil into the desert. Philo considers their flight into the desert to be a flight from women:

> For no Essene takes a wife, because a wife is a selfish creature, excessively jealous and an adept at beguiling the morals of her husband and seducing him by her continuing impostures ... For he who is either fast bound in the lures of his wife or under the stress of nature makes his children his first care ceases to be the

---

[6] Philo, *De Opif. Mund.* 151.

same to others and unconsciously becomes a different man and has passed from freedom into bondage.[7]

The negative view of sexuality expressed by Philo does not fit well with the Jewish views of his time or subsequently which praise and glory in sexual activity within marriage. Philo's negative attitude can almost be seen as blaming all human evils on sexual activity. 'The majority of wars,' he argues, 'and those the greatest, have arisen through amours and adulteries and the deceit of women'.[8]

Pleasure and sex were associated and so were sex and women, so it followed that men must reject all contact with women as they would woo men away from the pursuit of reason by their sexual charms. Philo praises virginity in men and women as being indispensable in the search for God and the development of the soul. Philo's views, as a Greek Jew who integrated Plato's philosophy with Hebrew thought, were to have a major influence and probably led to the development of the idea of Mary's virginity as representing her purity and her nearness to God. Someone who engaged in sexual activity would clearly not be a good exemplar of the perfect life. Indeed Philo himself says that 'It is meet that God should converse with the truly virgin nature'. It therefore made sense, and seemed fitting to the early Church, that Mary should be seen as a pure and holy woman who never had any sexual contact at all. (We can see echoes of this in today's society when it was considered essential that Prince Charles, as future heir to the British throne, should marry a virgin – hence, partly, the choice of Diana.)

Philo considered that the soul that seeks God (remembering Plato's influence, a person's identity is synonymous with his soul) is therefore that of a person who practices virginity. Philo praises older women who have voluntarily remained virgins. Physical virginity is seen by Philo as symbolizing spiritual virginity and nearness to God.

[7] Philo, *Apologia* 11.14–17.
[8] Philo, *Jos.* 55–57.

Philo was a crucial influence in combining the negative views of sexuality, arising from development of Jewish ideas on purity rituals, with the negativity of Plato's views of the body, to produce a wholly negative attitude to sex and the body among those early Church fathers who were influenced by a more philosophic approach to understanding Christianity. Bernard Hoose points to such an attitude in the writings of both the Roman theologian Tertullian (*c.* 160–*c.* 230), and St Jerome (*c.* 347–*c.* 419):

What is it, asked Tertullian, that all men and women do in both marriage and fornication? His answer was that they have sexual relations, and the desire to do so puts both marriage and fornication on the same footing ... St Jerome wrote that he praised marriage, but only because it caused virgins to be born. He gathered roses from thorns,[9] he said.

St Augustine of Hippo

Prior to St Augustine (354–430), Christians had developed tight rules regarding sexual expression. Unlike Jews, who had clear dietary laws as well as rules requiring circumcision to identify their community from those amongst whom they lived, Christians tended in the early centuries to rely on a severe sexual morality. Christians saw themselves as a 'holy people' a people set apart by God, rather like the 'chosen people' of Israel in the Old Testament. Just as the chosen people, the Jews, had signs of their 'separatedness' from the wider world in which they lived, so Christians sought a similar sign and found this in an emphasis on sexual purity. As Peter Brown says:

On the surface the Christian practised an austere sexual morality, easily recognizable and acclaimed by outsiders: total sexual

[9] Jerome, Epistles 22.20.

renunciation by the few; marital concord between the spouses, strong disapproval of remarriage. This surface was presented openly to outsiders ... Christians tended to make their exceptional sexual discipline bear the full burden of expressing the difference between themselves and the pagan world.[10]

It would be fair to say that some quarters of the early Christian Church developed an obsession about sex. For instance, one of the influential writers, St Basil of Caesarea, lists a number of sins with suitable penances. As Richard Price says:

> Violation of oaths is treated in two canons, thrift in two, participation in pagan or magical rites in five, murder or manslaughter in twelve and sexual offences in no less than forty-one. The length of penance is also indicative. Adultery and homosexual acts receive 15 years, which is more than the 10 years for abortion and only slightly less than the 20 years for wilful murder.[11]

The stress on sexual misdemeanours set out in these early writings continued throughout Christian history up until the present day. This may have been a legacy of the 'dirtiness' and lack of purity associated with sex in the Hebrew Scriptures. Even in the twentieth century, Christians tend to concentrate on sexual sins rather than, say, on economic or social injustice or on business morality. The seeds of the present obsession with sex were, therefore, sown at a very early date:

> ... we may conclude that at least until Augustine, the dominant factor in the development of a distinctive Christian sexual ethic was the need to express and preserve the purity of the Church as the body of Christ through the purity of the bodies of its

---

[10] Peter Brown, 'Late Antiquity', in P. Ariès and G. Duby, eds., *A History of Private Life*. Vol. 1 (ed. P. Veyne), 1987, p. 263.

[11] Richard Price, 'The Distinctiveness of Early Christian Sexual Ethics', *Heythrop Journal*, 1990, p. 261.

members ... Modern Christians who feel that traditional Christianity attached undue importance to sexual morality and made it too restrictive need to be aware that their own lack of sympathy with the traditional discipline arises not only from sexual liberation but also from a different ecclesiology, from a lowering of the boundaries between the Church and the world.[12]

The words 'until St Augustine' are highly significant here because Augustine was responsible for turning a generally negative attitude to sex which arose from a desire to maintain the identity of the growing Christian Church to a hostile environment into a negative attitude based on theological principles. St Augustine was the most influential of the early Christian theologians – he vigorously combated various heresies of his time and his ideas influenced not only early Councils of the Church but also Protestant reformers at the time of the Reformation.[13] One of the heretics he condemned was Jovinian, who maintained that there was no essential difference in holiness between the married and the celibate lives. Augustine wrote a powerful rejection of this in his book *The Good of Marriage*. 'It can in no way be doubted,' he wrote, 'that the chastity of continence is better than the chastity of marriage.'

The echoes of Philo's position here are strong. Augustine considered that sexual desire had to be tolerated, as an evil, since it was necessary for the procreation of children. When it was necessary to have sexual intercourse in order to produce children, the married couple could 'descend with a certain sadness' to their regrettable task.[14] A man who makes love to his wife because he wants to and not in order to procreate is, in Augustine's view, an 'adulterer' with his own wife, since sex involves lust.[15] Augustine distinguishes between feeling pleasure and enduring it which is

[12] Price, 'The Distinctiveness of Early Christian Sexual Ethics', p. 262.

[13] For a good introduction to Augustine see Richard Price, *Augustine*, Fount Christian Thinkers, Fount Paperbacks, 1996.

[14] Augustine, Sermon 51.15–25.348.

[15] Augustine, *Against Jovinian* 2.7.20

sinless, and seeking pleasure in sexual activity and enjoying it which is sinful. Gregory the Great (*c.* 540–603) likewise stated that 'legitimate carnal union ought to be for the sake of offspring, not pleasure, and for the sake of creating children, not of satisfying vices'.[16]

Price summarizes Augustine's position in saying:

> Augustine conceded to human weakness that men and women, without a very special gift of grace, cannot suppress their sexual drives; they need to exercise them, and this they can do without sin if they restrict sex to marriage. Ideally, all sex ought to be for the purpose of procreation. But such is the strength of the sexual drive that married couples are likely to have intercourse for the purposes of satisfying and assuaging their sexual urges. This is, of course, a sin; but if they only have sex within marriage and do not exclude procreation, their sin is only a minor one, easily forgiven.'[17]

The basis for Augustine's attitude was his recognition that sexual desire was not controllable by the will. He noted that male erections were not under rational control. Men could not have erections when they wanted to and indeed these sometimes occurred when they were not wanted.[18] Furthermore, 'wet dreams' occurred at night on occasion. Augustine therefore saw human genitalia (and he was specifically thinking of male rather than female genitalia) as being under the control of lust. He believed that lust was a consequence of original sin following Adam and Eve's expulsion from the Garden of Eden and that this was passed down from parent to child through the sexual act. Prior to Adam and Eve's expulsion, he maintained, men would have had full control over their sexual organs and procreation would have taken

---

[16] Gregory the Great, *In Gratian Decretum* 33.4.7.

[17] Price, *Augustine*, p. 68.

[18] This came to Augustine's attention when he visited the public baths as a young man and he had an erection in public to which his father drew attention as a mark of his son's virility. See also Augustine, *The City of God* 14.19.

place without erotic desire and purely by an act of the will.[19] The pleasure of the sexual act, due to orgasm, was, Augustine considered, so great that it overturned the power of reason and put men into the powers of 'female allurements'.[20]

Augustine devloped further the idea of concupiscence which has its origin in St Paul[21] – he held that this was due to the Fall and represented the desire for temporal desire independent of the control of reason.

Augustine emphasized the importance of fidelity in marriage. By this he meant that each partner had an obligation to satisfy the sexual needs of the other and responding to this duty was not sinful – rather it is the person who wants their needs satisfying who was sinful. This is vital – Augustine's views on this area were to have a considerable influence on thinking in the Middle Ages. Augustine does praise the companionship involved in marriage but he does not see this in any way as a central purpose. Augustine seemed to have little idea of friendship between marriage partners, indeed he considered that the first woman was only a fit helper for the first man because she could produce children. Another man would have been preferable if the aim was help in work, providing companionship or relief from solitude.[22]

Augustine's legacy was to cast a long shadow and to dominate thinking about sex in the Western Church for nearly seventeen hundred years. This legacy is well expressed by Peter Lombard:

> Whilst before sin man and woman could come together without the incentive of lust and the fire of concupiscence, and there would have been an 'undefiled bed' (Hebrews 13:4), the flesh was so corrupted in Adam through sin that after sin there could

---

[19] Augustine, *The City of God* 14.24.
[20] Augustine, *Soliloquies* 1.10. This was later endorsed by Aquinas, *Summa Theologiae* 2–2.151.4c.
[21] Ephesians 2:3; Romans 7:7ff.
[22] Augustine, *De Genesi ad Litteram* 9.5.

not have been carnal union without lustful concupiscence that is always a disability and even a fault unless it is excused by the goods of marriage. So the flesh formed into the body of a child is conceived in concupiscence and lust. Whence the flesh, which is conceived in corrupt concupiscence, is itself polluted and corrupted. Through contact with it the soul, when infused, contracts a stain by which it is polluted and becomes blameworthy. A stain, that is, which is the disability of concupiscence, which is original sin.[23]

Augustine's ideas on sex became more negative as he grew older – particularly as he was combating those who disagreed with him, most notably Julian, Bishop of Eclanum in Southern Italy. Julian was influenced by a Briton, Pelagius, who took a totally contrary view to Augustine as he did not consider that Adam and Eve's fall had subverted human free will. Pelagius had maintained that sexual desire could be controlled by the free decisions of human beings. Julian built on Pelagius' position maintaining that sex in itself was not bad, but it had to be controlled like all other desires. Julian challenged Augustine, for instance when he said that the sexual urge is:

> ... not some outstandingly good thing, but a drive placed in our bodies by God – a drive which you claim has been placed deep within us by the Devil, making your whole doctrine stand or fall upon little more than the discreet behaviour which surrounds the sexual act.[24]

Julian maintained that Augustine had a negative attitude to the human body stemming from his early years when he was closely identified with the Manichees (a sect characterized by a strongly dualistic philosophy and sexual renunciation). Augustine rejected this utterly and became more strident in his assertions. It was by no

[23] Peter Lombard, *Sentences* 2.31.4 (1. 506).
[24] Julian, *Opus Imperfectum* 3.142.1303, quoted in Peter Brown, *The Body and Society*, Faber and Faber, 1988.

means clear which of these two eminent theologians would win the day. Julian sought the support of an influential layman, Valerius, and Augustine wrote to Valerius rejecting Julian's position.[25]

Augustine can be easily misinterpreted – he did consider that chastity was the ideal but he did allow sex within marriage to be practised. In the end, it was Augustine's views which attained recognition and today more conservative scholars will maintain that the views of Pelagius and Julian were 'heretical'. However, what is heretical is simply the position that 'lost out' in the struggle between competing ideas, and this cannot be any sure indicator of truth. Indeed, even the most conservative modern scholars would reject many of Augustine's views – yet on these views much of Western society has traditionally based its views on sex.

Summary

Augustine's views were a culmination of ideas found in St Paul, in Platonic philosophy and in the writings of Philo of Alexandria, amongst others. He can be represented as saying that any sexual activity except that indulged in for the sole purpose of procreation is sinful. Sexuality is such a strong drive that it even resists the control of the will and can, therefore, be seen to have its origin in the Fall from perfection after the dismissal of Adam and Eve from the Garden of Eden. Certainly sex outside marriage is totally rejected but even sex within marriage should be avoided unless it is necessary to produce children – and then it should not be enjoyed.

[25] Augustine, *On Marriage and Concupiscence*.

SIX

Natural Law
and the Middle Ages

The Middle Ages

Many medieval writers discussed issues in the sexual arena, and a broad consensus emerged which was promulgated by confessors and others. There was considerable interest in sexual rules in general following the requirement, promulgated in 1215, that all members of the Western Christian Church should make a personal confession to a priest at least once a year.

Throughout the Middle Ages, sex was considered as evil unless it was excused by marriage. Marriage, in turn, was seen as a way of procreating and also as a way of avoiding the danger of lust by providing a legitimate outlet for sexual desire. Sexual activity of all kinds was best avoided, and sex was held to be incompatible with prayer.

Medieval writers constantly stressed the 'debt' that one marriage partner had to pay to the other. This had nothing to do with love but was a purely sexual debt which enabled one partner in the marriage to satisfy their sexual needs on the body of the other partner, irrespective of that partner's inclinations.[1] If one partner refused to agree to sex then it might lead the other partner into sin – this idea comes from St Paul's saying 'that it is better to marry than to burn' (with desire) – and if the one partner refuses sexual access to the other then the first person may be led into sin. The man could not request intercourse when the women had a period – this

[1] Cf. 'The Marital debt' in Pierre Payer, *The Bridling of Desire*, University of Toronto Press, 1993.

was the one time in which a woman did not commit a sin if she refused access to her husband. If a woman's husband insisted on sexual access in order to avoid sinning (either by masturbation or by adultery) then this was a minor matter:

> If someone has the intention of using intercourse to avoid fornication on his own part, then this is a venial sin, for marriage was not intended for that although one may engage sinlessly in intercourse to prevent fornication by one's spouse since this is a matter of pursuing one's duty.[2]

Both Alexander of Hales and William of Rennes clearly state that a wife has no right to refuse her husband, even if this means that the husband has to take the wife by force. However, Alexander of Hales states: 'The married are bound not to ask at certain times, nevertheless if asked they are bound to repay.'[3] These 'times' at which sexual intercourse could not be requested by a marriage partner were quite extensive — they included all holy days and the eves of feast days; forty days in Lent and eight days after Easter; forty days in Advent and eight days after Christmas; eight days before Pentecost; Sundays (as this was the day Jesus rose from the dead), Fridays (as this was the day Jesus died) and, in the case of some theologians, Saturdays (because this day was dedicated to the Virgin Mary) and Thursdays (as this was the date of the last supper) as well as five days before communion.[4]

Impotence, either male or female, was a ground for an annulment of marriage provided the impotence existed at the time of marriage. Detailed discussion took place amongst theologians as to different types of impotence and whether this was temporary or permanent and whether it related to all partners as well as the circumstance in which impotence could allow a marriage to be annulled.

[2] Aquinas, *Summa Theologiae Suppl.* 49.a5.ad2.
[3] Alexander of Hales, Glossa in 4 *Sent.* 32.9.
[4] For detailed discussion see Payer, *The Bridling of Desire*, pp. 98–102.

Aquinas and Natural Law

St Thomas Aquinas (1226–1274) was one of the greatest theologians and philosophers in the history of Christianity. He was a professor at the University of Paris at a particularly significant time. Many volumes of the writings of Aristotle had been lost in the West but they had been preserved in the centres of Islamic learning in Persia. These writings became available in Paris shortly before Aquinas took up his post. His great contribution was to use the philosophy of Aristotle to arrive at moral and religious teachings which were in accordance with the tradition which was then broadly accepted. Aristotle's philosophy is meant to be empirically based – in other words it is claimed to start from experience of the world in which human beings live. Much of his understanding of morality stems from an examination of the nature of human beings.

Aquinas' philosophic understanding of morality and sex is particularly significant as, after some initial hesitancy, it became accepted as normative within Western Christianity and has been passed down today through the Roman Catholic tradition (although many Protestant theologians, as we shall see, would have considerable reservations about it and some modern Catholic theologians now have reservations about it).

Aquinas was committed to a search for truth. He believed that the search for understanding about God and human morality was of fundamental importance and that truth could be sought – it was not simply a human construct. Starting from the general injunction that good should be sought and evil avoided, Aquinas unpacks the good in terms of some very general primary precepts which he obtains by looking at the *telos* or purpose of human life. He considers that human beings are social animals made by God to live together and to render each other assistance. They should seek to live, work, reproduce, educate children, have an ordered society and worship God. These precepts are very general, but Aquinas then goes on to outline them in considerably more detail.

It is important to note at the outset that Aquinas follows Aristotle's teleological approach to ethics – in other words he seeks to work from the evidence of experience regarding the purpose of human life or parts of the human body to determine what is and is not right. He also assumes that all human beings share a common human nature, so one can work from general principles which will, because of the shared nature, apply to all human beings without exception. Some of the norms arrived at using Aquinas' approach are termed deontological, since they do not admit exceptions and apply in all times and in all cultures.

Aquinas' methodology of looking at purpose or *telos* is followed when it comes to reproduction. He considers that the *telos* of genitalia is procreation. This may at first seem an obvious reply, but if it is accepted, then various consequences follow:

* No artificial methods of birth control can be employed since this frustrates the purpose of the sexual act – which is procreation.
* Masturbation is sinful since this means using genitalia (whether male or female) for a purpose for which they are not intended, namely pleasure or the release of sexual tension, and in no sense is this act open to the possibility of procreation.
* Homosexuality, if it is practised, is intrinsically evil since it is to use genitalia for a purpose for which they are not intended since procreation cannot result and homosexuality is 'against nature'.
* Sex can never have pleasure or the expression of love as its main object since, again, this means using genitalia for a purpose for which they were not intended.

Aquinas' views were adopted, almost without qualification, by the medieval Roman Catholic Church. Even today, in documents such as the recent encyclical *Veritatis Splendor* (1993), his views are confirmed and endorsed – although the unitive side of sexual activity (i.e. uniting a married couple) is now listed as a purpose for sexual intercourse as well as the traditional procreative function. However, Thomist (i.e. Aquinas') views on sexuality, when analysed in detail, are clearly a product of his time – although it can be argued that his basic methodology still has a great deal to teach us.

In particular, Aquinas makes assumptions which at first appear reasonable but which can be readily challenged. For example, he assumes that all human beings share a common human nature given by God. Aquinas' approach to ethics involves working out what human nature should be. Any human who does not share this nature is then considered to 'fall short' and to be defective.[5] If someone, for instance, is sexually attracted to members of the same sex, then they have a defective human nature – Aquinas considers that they are not as they 'should be'. Such an inclination is not in itself sinful, it represents an 'evil suffered' rather than an 'evil done' and it would only become sinful if the inclination is practised.

This idea of a single human nature (on which the whole Natural Law approach to ethics rests) is rejected by many today who argue that each individual is genetically distinct. Some may be homosexually inclined and some heterosexually whilst others may be inclined to both sexes. Mary Midgley rejects the idea that there is a single human nature and also the idea that any nature can be described as particularly and distinctly human – because so much of human nature has close parallels in the animal world.[6] Gareth Moore (like Aquinas, a member of the Dominican Order) maintains that what we regard as human nature is a product of the society and culture in which we live.[7] It is *we* who pick out those features which *we* want to maintain are held in common and which represent human nature as *we* consider it should be, and it is *we* who decide which features to ignore (such as hair and eye colour, height, etc.). Nowhere does this apply more than in the case of sexuality, where it is *we* who decide what is normal as a way of ruling our behaviour which to *us* appears abnormal.

[5] Cf. Peter Vardy, *The Puzzle of Evil*, Fount Paperbacks, 1992, chapter 2.
[6] Mary Midgley, *Beast and the Man: The Root of Human Nature*, Cornell University Press, 1978.
[7] Moore, *Body in Context*, p. 33.

Aquinas maintains that marriage must be monogamous and indissoluble and that all sexual acts should only be undertaken for the purpose of procreation, which follows from his definition of the assumed purpose of genitalia.[8] A marriage without sex would, according to Aquinas, be preferable to a marriage with sex. He does not consider sex itself as evil, provided – and only provided – it is directed towards procreation. Apart from Aquinas' claim that there is a single human nature, he may be held to be mistaken in saying, for instance that:

1 God implanted male souls at 40 days and female souls at 90 days in the developing foetus – Aquinas took this idea from Aristotle. This position continued to be accepted until the seventeeth century and is today universally regarded as false. The whole idea of the implantation of souls is fraught with problems and, indeed, is something that the Roman Catholic Church itself no longer emphasizes. If this was accepted, of course, a foetus at less than this period would then not be human, and indeed Aquinas considered this to be the case. If someone injures a woman and she has a miscarriage then provided the foetus is less than 90 or 40 days the person injuring the woman would not be held to have committed murder. Even if, as the Catholic Church hundreds of years later came to hold, souls were implanted at conception, this does not establish identity as we now know that after the sperm has entered the egg, the fertilized egg can divide for up to 14 days or, once having divided, can again come together. The position is, at best, confused.[9]

2 All babies would be male, taking after the perfect prototype of the father. However, this is sometimes prevented by the adverse influence of 'a moist south wind' and a female foetus results.[10] A woman is a 'misbegotten foetus'.[11] It is, perhaps, unfair on

[8] Aquinas, *Summa contra Gentiles* 123/4.
[9] For further discussion see Vardy & Grosch, *The Puzzle of Ethics*, chapter 12.
[10] *Summa Theologiae* 1.92.1.
[11] *Summa Theologiae* 1.92.1 ob.1, ad.1.

Aquinas to quote such a ludicrous example, but his error here points to his possible fallibility in other areas and this is often not accepted.

3 Women are less rational, less suited to intellectual pursuits and less capable of firm judgements than men. They should, therefore, be subject to men, who are 'wiser than themselves'.[12]

4 Sex itself is necessary to propagate the species but it has adverse effects on the search for truth and, therefore, celibacy or, in the case of women, virginity, are to be preferred as these enable one to 'contemplate the things of God and this was conducive to the good of the soul'.[13]

5 Sex during a woman's period may, if it involves conception, harm the resultant child which may be born deformed.[14]

6 Rape is a less serious sin than masturbation, as at least in the case of rape the genitalia are being used for their proper purpose and conception may result. Masturbation, however, misuses genitalia as there is no possibility of conception and is a mortal sin.

7 It is sinful to seek sex in marriage unless the intention is to procreate, although it is a far worse sin to have sex outside marriage.[15]

Although marriage is not the ideal state, Aquinas does recognize and hold in high regard the love between husband and wife and considers that marriage can be a sign of Christ's presence to the Church – provided the marriage is of permanently committed Christians who are dedicated to having children, bringing them up and doing good works.[16]

[12] *Summa Theologiae* 1.92.1. Also 11.11.156.1; *Suppl.* 64.5, *Summa contra Gentiles* 3/11.123.
[13] *Summa Theologiae Suppl.* 49.1; 65.5.
[14] *Summa Theologiae Suppl.* 64.3.
[15] *Summa Theologiae Suppl.* 49. 1.
[16] *Summa Theologiae Suppl.* 49.1:49; 65.5; *Summa Theologiae* 11–11.26.11.

Aquinas recognizes that male and female are complementary, but also sees the female as naturally subservient to the male – women are created to be subject to men. They are inferior both because they are 'defective males' and also because they are passive in the sexual act. (Many today, of course, would question this.) However Aquinas does seem to consider that after death women and men will be treated equally dependent on their merits.[17]

Aquinas maintained that any form of sexual activity that was not conventional (in terms of position) and 'normal' and did not allow the possibility of conception was always a mortal sin.[18] What is more, reason is weighed down by sexual activity and, therefore, any sexual activity undermines the human being's ability to act rationally and to draw closer to God: 'Since coitus weighs down reason because of carnal pleasure, it renders men inept for spiritual things.'[19]

The Council of Trent (1545–63) was important in confirming Aquinas' approach to sexual morality. It also strengthened the grip of the Church by insisting not just on confession but on sins being reported with details on the kind of sin committed, the number of times committed and the circumstances under which the sins were committed. This led to even more detailed rules being formulated as priests and confessors became interested in the precise details of sexual misdemeanours and grave sexual sins so that they could advise the person on the salvation of their soul from the fires of hell.

Lessons to be Learned from the Middle Ages

What relevance have these speculations to an understanding of sexual morality today? The reason for dwelling on these matters here is to show the extent to which theologians and spiritual

[17] *Summa Theologiae Suppl.* 64.5; 81.4.
[18] Aquinas, 4 *Sent.* 31 and *Summa Theologiae* 2–2.154.11.
[19] *Summa Theologiae Suppl.* 64.5.

advisers in this crucial period for the development of moral ideas went into considerable detail on the acceptability of certain types of sexual behaviour and there was broad agreement as to what was and what was not permissible. In particular, the idea of sexual activity as a 'debt' that one partner was bound to pay to the other was central.

Aquinas, of course, had no idea of a woman's cycle or her fertility, no idea of the union of sperm and egg or of other biological details. Certainly he cannot be blamed for such lack of knowledge – but when his ideas are taken as normative and as still having direct relevance when so many of them are based on entirely false assumptions, this raises questions about the validity of ethical teaching erected on such unsure foundations. Effectively, the Roman Catholic Church has gradually abandoned the teachings of Aquinas in so far as they have come to be shown to be unacceptable. The question is only how far this will go – as yet it has not extended far into the sexual arena.

Aquinas used Church tradition combined with the latest philosophic thinking to come to significant conclusions about sexual morality. If he had been writing today, he would have been similarly concerned with a passionate search for truth – using all the latest psychological, philosophical and theological understanding. He would be very unlikely to rest content with Aristotle when so much more work has been done in philosophy; he would have taken on board the excellent work done by many biblical theologians today and all that psychologists and sociologists can tell us about the nature of the human person.

Aquinas' basic methodology, which involved a search for truth and a proper understanding of human nature, may still provide a valuable model even for those who dismiss his conclusions. This book will follow in Aquinas' footsteps in the search for a truthful account of sexual ethics, but it will also attempt to take into account the enormous developments in our understanding of human beings and their sexuality since the thirteenth century.

SEVEN

The Orthodox Perspective

The Christian Church remained united for a thousand years – the Councils of the early Church hammered out, during the first 500 years, the exact nature of Christian doctrine. These Councils were often full of political intrigue and the debates were fierce. Sometimes quick votes were taken to prevent parties of bishops delayed on their journey to the Council from voting. Sometimes opponents were locked up to prevent their voting against certain proposals. Remarkably, however, in spite of this all-too-human intrigue, the Church remained united. To be sure, there were many heresies that arose but these were eventually rejected and the mainstream Church held on to a unified vision of doctrine and theology.

The first major and permanent split occurred in 1054, although the origins of the split extended back for several centuries. It was in 1054 that the Western Church centred on Rome and the Eastern Church centred on Constantinople (the modern Istanbul) split. This split is still with us in the divide between the Orthodox and Roman Catholic Churches. Both of these bodies, however, respect the antiquity and the traditions of the other, as well as the extent to which they can both claim to authentically represent elements of the mainstream Christian heritage. It is, indeed, one of the major objectives of the present leadership of the Western Church to bring the Western and Eastern Churches back together in unity. The Orthodox understanding of sexuality and marriage is, therefore, of crucial importance.

The Orthodox approach is particularly significant as it tends to attach much greater importance to the teachings of the early

67

Church Fathers and was not influenced by Aristotle and Scholastic philosophy, nor by the legacy of St Augustine, in the way in which the Roman Catholic Church has been. Fr John Meyendorff puts the position of the early Church like this:

> The Christian Church, both at the time of persecution and during her alliance with the Roman state, accepted the Roman laws regarding marriage ... conformity with Roman concepts and terminology is found in the writings of the Early Fathers ... Their meaning is not that the Church was indifferent to the issue of marriage ... Christians understood the value of the Roman order. They appreciated the progress which some aspects of Roman Law were introducing in human relations.[1]

Meyendorff rightly recognizes here that the view of marriage held by the early Church was heavily influenced by that of the Roman state – particularly when Christianity became the official religion of the Roman empire. The Roman idea of marriage was of a unity freely entered into by free individuals.

A Christian marriage is *both* a legal agreement between a man and a woman *and*, theologically, it also became accepted, albeit not initially, as a sacrament – a pathway towards salvation – in which the man and woman bind themselves together 'in the most profoundly indissoluble manner'.[2] The Western Church considers marriage to be a sacrament (a sacrament is defined by Aquinas as 'a sign of a holy thing, insofar as it sanctifies man'[3]). In a marriage it is the bridal couple who administer the sacraments to each other – they do this before the priest, but the priest is not, strictly, necessary. The couple make promises to each other and the priest's words declare what has happened but it is the couple's own declarations, not those of the priest, which are decisive. In the early years of the Christian

---

[1] John Meyendorff, *Marriage: An Orthodox Perspective*, St Vladimir's Seminary Press, 1984, pp. 17–18.
[2] *Familiaris Consortio Vatican*, 1981, p. 13n.
[3] Aquinas, *On Sacraments in the Community*, 3.q. 60.a. 2.

Church, priests had no role at all to play in marriage until the fourth century. Indeed Jerome rejected this:

> A preacher on continence should not celebrate weddings.[4]

but as early as the second century Ignatius of Antioch had maintained that Christian couples should only marry with the consent of the bishop:

> In order that the marriage should be according to the Lord and not according to desire.[5]

Over the centuries, a distinctive Christian understanding of marriage developed, although there was a divergence between Eastern and Western Christianity as to the role of the priest and how marriage as a sacrament should be understood. In the West, the Catholic Church maintained in the Council of Trent that all marriages represent a sacrament, even those not performed before a Catholic priest.[6] In this tradition, feelings of love are irrelevant – there is no reference to marital love as a condition for the validity of the sacrament of marriage. A marriage in the Catholic Church cannot be brought to an end – except by annulment. Annulment has the great advantage of allowing those involved, subject to the approval of the Church, to recognize that what appeared to be a marriage was not one at all. Once an annulment is granted, it is as if the parties had never been married at all. Under Catholic Canon Law, detailed rules have been worked out as to the circumstance under which a marriage may be annulled. These include the following:

1 If one or other of the parties to the marriage did not know what they were doing and went through the ceremony without being properly informed of the consequences of their act.

[4] Quoted in Price, 'The Distinctiveness of Early Christian Sexual Ethics', p. 271.
[5] Cf. Price, 'The Distinctiveness of Early Christian Sexual Ethics', p. 271.
[6] See footnote references to declarations by Pope Pius IX and by Pope Leo XIII in Helmut Theilecke, *The Ethics of Sex*, James Clarke, London, 1964, p. 128n.

2 If one or other of the parties to the marriage did not intend to have children (and since propagation has traditionally been held to be one of main purposes of marriage this is held to render the marriage invalid).

3 If one or other of the parties had entered the marriage with insufficient preparation or thought.

4 If one or other of the parties was, at the time of the marriage, unable to sustain the obligations of the marriage relationship.

The ideal of Christian marriage is that it should be permanent and indissoluble, however this is an ideal and the Orthodox Church, unlike the Catholic, recognizes that it is not always obtainable. Human beings are often sinful and live in a fallen world. The Orthodox Church recognizes two important distinctions:

- The difference between the ideal of an indissoluble marriage and the reality of human failure and sinfulness, and
- The difference between the theological ideal and the reality of divorce in the world.

These distinctions are vital because they result in a significantly different approach by the Orthodox and Roman Catholic Church to many areas of human sexuality – and the Orthodox Church can claim equal (if not greater) length of tradition for its views. What is more, its views were the views of the united Christian Church up to the time of the split between the West and the East.

The early Church considered marriage as primarily a secular matter – it was the Eucharist that showed the real unity between the man and the woman. As Meyendorff says (referring to the period after the fourth century):

Every Christian couple desirous of marriage went through the formalities of civil registration, which gave it validity in secular society; and then through their joint participation in the regular

Sunday liturgy, in the presence of the entire local Christian community, they received the Bishop's blessing. It was then that their civil agreement became also 'sacrament', with eternal value.[7]

The main difference between the Roman Catholic and the Orthodox view of marriage lies in the centrality of the Eucharist to the Orthodox. Up to the ninth century, the Christian Church had no rite of marriage separate from the Eucharist. The Roman Catholic Church has, through its Canon Law, put itself into the position of a legal body with its own firm rules. It is, as set out above, the man and woman who enter into an indissoluble contract or covenant and the priest is only the witness of this. Even after the wedding ceremony it is not until the man and woman have made love (defined as the man coming inside or penetrating the woman) that the marriage is considered to have taken place. A marriage in Church that is not subsequently consummated is not a marriage at all. On this view, as the couple enter into an indissoluble contract, no one can dissolve it.

The Orthodox Church, by contrast, considers the priest to be the minister of the marriage and, as the marriage is essentially a sacrament, it is, from the Church's viewpoint, more a theological mystery than a legal contract. In Orthodoxy, the marriage is a civil matter and the sacrament of the Eucharist is a 'Crowning' recognition of the marriage before God.[8] Meyendorff points out that, under the Communist governments in Eastern Europe where no marriages could take place in church, there was no problem in a couple getting married in a civil ceremony and then attending a

---

[7] Meyendorff, *Marriage*, pp. 21–2.

[8] The 'Crowning' dates from the fourth century and is a blessing ceremony accompanied by a brief prayer during the liturgy of the Eucharist. It was not until the tenth century that a 'crowning' service separate from the Eucharist was recognized. The 'crowns' which are placed on the head of the groom and bride recall those crowns with which Christian martyrs are crowned in heaven.

normal Eucharist because the presence of the couple at the Eucharist was the key theological element in uniting the couple.[9] The marriage is not valid in the eyes of the Orthodox Church until they have received Communion.

The marriage is a legal contract from the point of view of the State but not of the Church. If a marriage breaks down, then this may be an occasion of sin but it is not a legal contract which has been broken under Church Law. The Orthodox Church is concerned with the forgiveness of sin and bringing people to salvation. It considers, therefore, that divorce can occur (like any other form of human failing) but that life must go on and it may well be right that the parties to the marriage should get married again.

The Orthodox Church recognizes that children are a part of marriage but does not emphasize the centrality of procreation in the 'Crowning' service. Rather the emphasis is on God's blessing on the couple themselves. The Orthodox also have a positive attitude to marriage and have not had the sometimes negative view of sexuality common in the past in the Western tradition.

Remarriage after Divorce

The Orthodox Church has always been concerned to ensure that marriage is a freely chosen agreement entered into by two individuals, but it does accept that a marriage may break down and come to an end. The early Church recognized this:

Divorce by simple mutual consent was tolerated up to a law issued by emperor Theodosius II in 449 which forbade it, but it was again authorized by Justin II in 566. The law of Justin II was repealed only in the eighth century. Throughout all that period, divorce, with right of remarriage, was granted not only on the grounds of adultery, but also on such grounds as political treason, planning of murder, disappearance for five years or

[9] Meyendorff, *Marriage*, p. 24.

more, unjustified accusation of adultery and, finally, monastic vows of one of the partners.[10]

Not a single Father of the early Church ever questioned these rules. The united Christian Church remained faithful to the New Testament ideal of indissoluble marriage but accepted that human beings might fail to live up to this ideal. Marriage failure is sinful and, if it occurs, a period of penance is required, but after this period a second, and even, exceptionally, a third marriage could be approved. However, only the first marriage was blessed by the Church during the Eucharist. Divorce and remarriage is tolerated as a concession to human weakness and certainly not as something to be welcomed. The Orthodox Church considers that marriage continues after death and, therefore, requires penance even when a second marriage takes place after the death of the first partner.

A second marriage can take place in Church, although the person who was previously married cannot take Communion and will generally be forbidden to take Communion for two years. The second marriage service is significantly different from the first being shorter and simpler and with an emphasis on asking for 'forgiveness for transgressions' and for 'pardon'. Even the great figures of the Old Testament to whom reference is made in the service are different – the second marriage refers to Rahab the prostitute (Joshua 2:1–24), the penitent tax collector (Luke 18:10–14) and the good thief (Luke 23:40–43). All these receive God's forgiveness through faith and this is clearly appropriate to a second marriage. In fact, the stress on penitence is so great that Meyendorff questions whether it is suitable for use on the happy occasion which a marriage should be – however, its theological point is clear and significant.

Effectively, therefore, the Orthodox Church, like the Catholic Church, considers divorce and remarriage to be sinful and a human failure which requires penance. However, in the eyes of the

<hr>

[10] Meyendorff, *Marriage*, p. 56.

Orthodox tradition, this does not invalidate the second (or, exceptionally, third) marriage, but it does demand penance and the divorced party absenting him or herself from the Eucharist for a period of years. The Orthodox Church's aim, as that of the early Church, is to give human beings who have failed a second chance.

Contraception

The Orthodox Church did not agree with the view held by the Catholic Church up to the Second Vatican Council in 1965 that the main purpose of marriage or sexual activity is procreation or with the post-Council view of that 'unitive' and 'procreative' functions of sexual acts within marriage may not be separated. Marriage in the Orthodox Church is considered as an end in itself – a unity between man and woman paralleling the unity between Christ and the Church. Meyndorff puts the point well:

> ... until quite recently, Western thought on sex and marriage was entirely and almost exclusively dominated by the teaching of St Augustine (d. 430). The peculiarity of Augustine's point of view was that he considered sex and sexual instinct as the channel through which the guilt for the 'original sin' of Adam was transferred to Adam's posterity. Marriage, therefore, was itself sinful in as much as it presupposed sex, and could be justified only 'through childbirth'. Consequently, if childbirth is artificially prevented, sexual intercourse – even in lawful marriage – is fundamentally sinful.

> The Orthodox Church ... recognizes the sanctity of St Augustine, but his doctrinal authority in Orthodoxy is far from being as absolute as it used to be in the West ...[11]

[11] Meyendorff, *Marriage*, p. 60.

The Orthodox Church does not consider that, in itself, celibacy is to be preferred to sexual activity, nor does it consider that a distinction should be drawn between 'artificial' and 'natural' means of birth control. Instead it leaves the question of birth control to be decided by the conscience of individual couples.

Married Clergy

The Roman Catholic Church, as we have seen, has taken a strong stand against married clergy since shortly after the time of the split with the Orthodox.[12] However, the early tradition of the united Church allowed married clergy and the Orthodox Church has remained faithful to this – provided that the man was married before becoming ordained. The Church maintains that candidates for ordination must be stable and mature and it does not consider that entry into marriage after ordination is compatible with these requirements. Orthodox bishops, however, may not be married, because a bishop has to devote himself wholly to his flock and this is incompatible with marriage.

Again the reason for the difference between the Orthodox and Roman Catholic Churches is, historically, due to the Orthodox remaining faithful to the early Church fathers and not giving such influence to Augustine and the scholastic philosophy of Aquinas. The Orthodox have not imbued sex and marriage with the negative connotations found in much Western theology.

Integrity in Life

The Orthodox Church recognizes the legitimacy of both the married and celibate lifestyle, but considers that either state must be lived authentically and with integrity. Orthodox Canon Law puts it like this:

[12] AD 1074 in Rome and 1139 for the rest of the Western Church.

> ... apart from celibacy and marriage there is no other irre-
> proachable situation. Do you desire to marry? You must observe
> the laws of marriage. You do not like to marry? Then practice
> celibacy, but do not adulterate marriage and do not make a
> pretence of celibacy.

In other words, integrity in one's chosen path is required. The
Orthodox have always had a positive attitude to marriage and sexual
activity in marriage – St John Chrysostom (307–407), one of
the leading theologians who have greatly influenced the Orthodox
Church, wrote that a couple when truly united were an image of
God. It is true that the monastic tradition was even stronger in the
Eastern Church than in the Western, but combined with this went
a positive attitude to those who chose the marriage path. Indeed,
some Orthodox theologians have seen sexual love as the basis for
spiritual progress[13] – as have some more recent Western theologians.
This positive view of love was an outgrowth of a similar positive
attitude that developed in Jewish teaching and was very different
from the Western Christian approach.

Orthodox Canon Law also addresses the issue of cohabitation
and makes clear that cohabitation cannot be the same as marriage. Nevertheless, the Church's wording is muted and does not
condemn cohabitation, saying only that it cannot be equivalent to
marriage:

> We now also order that marriages be confirmed with a sacred
> blessing, and if the couple will neglect that procedure, their
> cohabitation will not be considered at any time as marriage and
> will not produce the legal effects of marriage.

Here again can be seen the separation between marriage as a state
institution and the blessing which is the Church's contribution and

---

[13] Vladimir Soloviev maintained this in 'The Meaning of Love', quoted by
Mary Anne Oliver, *Conjugal Spirituality*, Sheed & Ward, 1994, p. 25.

is crucially required for the marriage to be valid in the eyes of the Church. However, there is no condemnation of cohabitation – just a recognition that this cannot be the same as marriage.

Summary

The Orthodox approach to sexuality, marriage and divorce is faithful to the practice of the early Church. It does not condemn birth control and sees the central purpose of sex as unitive. It sets forth the Christian ideal but is tolerant of human sin and weakness and, after a period of penance, is prepared to accept the realities of human life which include divorce and remarriage. The Orthodox approach may be considered to have always affirmed the importance of integrity and personal responsibility in the chosen form of life, but without any sense that sexuality or marriage is in any sense evil or second best.

EIGHT

The Reformation

After the split between the Western and Eastern Churches in the eleventh century, the Protestant Reformation of the sixteenth century saw the Western Church itself divided still further. The Protestant Reformers and the new churches they helped to found rejected or modified Roman Catholic teaching on many issues of sexuality, particularly on clerical celibacy and the status and purpose of marriage.

Reformation Thinkers

Erasmus (c. 1466–1536)

Erasmus was a close friend of Thomas More (1477–1535). They were both true Europeans, travelling widely in a world where boundaries were of little significance to scholars and where ideas were discussed freely and openly. They were also passionately concerned with the good for humanity, and their views coincided to a considerable degree. They were part of a widespread European intellectual movement called 'humanism', but this was a Christian humanism which had as its aim the just and peaceful ordering of society.[1] This may seem surprising as Thomas More was to be martyred by Henry VIII because of his refusal to admit the king's authority over the Church in England, whilst Erasmus is thought of as one of the great Reformers, anticipating many of the ideas later

[1] See Anne Murphy, *Thomas More*, Fount Christian Thinkers, Fount Paperbacks, 1996.

put forward by Luther while still remaining a member of the Catholic Church.

Muriel Porter has written an excellent account of the changes in attitudes and rules relating to clergy marriage which took place at the time of the Reformation. She says that:

> Erasmus offered a vision of marriage that is positive, warm and attractive ... Erasmus claimed it as his central proposition that the state of marriage was of a value equal to that of celibacy. He was rapidly criticized as a heretic for such a preposterous claim, a claim he nevertheless defended.[2]

Erasmus went as far as to describe the unmarried state as unnatural and claimed that sexuality was intrinsic to God's creation and should therefore be looked on as a good. What is most distinctive is that he accepts married sexuality for the purpose of pleasure as at least a minor part of marriage – thus marking a tremendous shift from the tradition that had preceded him and, indeed, a departure from the suspicion of sex which the Protestant Reformers were to hold. Erasmus held that marriage was primarily for companionship and for mutual 'solace', as well as for the production of children. Bringing both these elements together placed him centuries in advance of Church thinking and made him subject to severe attack.

Erasmus strongly advocated the marriage of clergy – partly because he saw so many clergy who claimed to be celibate but were, in fact, secretly married or living with housekeepers or other women. He thought this was a mockery and a travesty as well as a denial of the humanity of women. Both Erasmus and Thomas More had a high view of women – both were married and in both cases they treated their wives with love and respect.

[2] Muriel Porter, *Sex, Marriage and the Church*, Dove, 1996, pp. 41–2.

Luther (1483–1546)

Martin Luther was one of the most influential Christian thinkers – his reaction against the accepted teaching of the Church laid the groundwork for much subsequent Protestant theology and also provided an alternative understanding to the approach stemming from Aquinas – although Luther himself was influenced by and educated within this framework.[3] Interpreting Luther's views is not an easy task. Marriage is a 'holy estate and divine ordinance' and a 'vocation' through which the division of gender roles in the creation can be overcome to provide an avenue back to God. What is more, sex and birth fill him with wonder:

> ... it is most worthy of wonder that a woman receives semen ... which is given shape and nourished until the foetus is ready for breathing air. When the foetus has been brought into the world ... no new nourishment appears, but ... from the two breasts, as from a fountain, there flows milk by which a baby is nourished. All these developments afford the fullest occasion for wonderment and are wholly beyond our understanding.[4]

Luther's thought operated within this framework. Lisa Cahill points out that Luther's apparently positive attitude to marriage is somewhat tempered. He says that only a few people are exempt from the command to marriage either because of their physical condition or, very rarely indeed, because they have a genuine call to celibacy. Cahill recognizes that this is in tension with the ending of *The Estate of Marriage* which says:

> Intercourse is never without sin, but God excuses it by his grace because the estate of marriage is his work, and he preserves in and through the sin all that good which he has implanted and blessed in marriage.

[3] For a clear introduction to Luther's thought see Hans-Peter Grosshans, *Luther*, Fount Christian Thinkers, Fount Paperbacks, 1997.
[4] Luther, *Lectures on Genesis, Luther's Works*, vol. 1, p. 126.

Cahill comments:

> This passage suggests some questions. Why is the sexual act always sinful if it is part of God's ordinance and command? Is God a cosmic utilitarian who commands sin that good may result? How can God command a sinful act, then 'excuse' it? Indeed, why is it in need of excuse if it is commanded and the avenue through which the promise of creation is fulfilled? Is Luther by means of this paradox articulating a theologically coherent position? Or is it another instance of his notorious disinterest in systematic thought, as well as a remnant of an Augustinian and unbiblical negativity towards all sexual activity?[5]

Luther was generally negative about celibacy saying that the spiritual life of most men is 'wretched' and 'un-Christian, vain and pernicious'. Luther himself decided to marry, yet in his writings he refers to sexual desire and making love as occasions of 'shame' and 'disgust'.[6] He treats marriage and sexuality with much more suspicion than Erasmus, and was more heavily influenced by the past Christian tradition. However, he is positive about women in saying: 'Men can't do without women. Even if it were possible for men to beget children, they still couldn't do without women.'

Luther rejected the idea that marriage was a sacrament. He reserved the term sacrament for holy events laid down in the Bible and considered that to claim marriage as a sacrament was a human invention. The rite of marriage is, essentially, a civil ceremony in which the Church is not of vital importance. Marriage, he maintained, was ordained for all human beings and not just for Christians. The only role of the Church, Luther believed, was to bless the civil ceremony of marriage. In fact, Luther has good theological grounds for claiming this as up until the tenth century marriage was performed by lay people and for the next two centuries marriages

[5] Cahill, *Between the Sexes*, p. 124.
[6] Luther, *Lectures on Genesis*, pp. 62–3, 71, 105, 117, 118, 142.

were performed outside the church. Later still, priests were involved, but still the marriage took place outside the church.

Luther's own marriage on 13 June 1525 was performed in his home. The marriage was, it is true, blessed by a priest, but this blessing did not make the marriage. This is significant, because civil marriage (to which so many Christians today take exception) has been the general practice for most of Christian history.

Luther's teaching about divorce was motivated by his concern for the situations in which human beings find themselves. He considered marriage to be indissoluble but was prepared to allow exceptions to this when the action of one partner to a marriage makes life intolerable for the other – for instance: adultery, desertion, a refusal of sexual access, or if the Christian partner is forced into an un-Christian way of life. Luther also accepted the possibility of remarriage if a separated person is refused reconciliation by the former partner and is unable to remain celibate. He maintained that remarriage is acceptable on the grounds that 'God will not demand the impossible'. Luther's ethics were primarily practical. As Cahill says, Luther:

> ... constantly tests Christian theory and practice by their power to transform the brokenness, pain and even tedium of daily affairs. His norm is an experience of faith fruitful to humanity, piety, forgiveness and works of love.[7]

Having said this, Luther is realistic in recognizing that marriages do not always remain happy but he maintains that it may be better to suffer in an unhappy marriage with Christian fortitude rather than to seek release. Such suffering can, he argues, provide a road to heaven.

In many ways, the approach of Luther and Aquinas have similarities in that they take Church tradition seriously and yet fit this in to the experience of human life in their own time. However, whereas

---

[7] Cahill, *Between the Sexes*, p. 133.

Aquinas gave priority to Aristotle's philosophy, Luther gives priority to the Bible, and is willing to take a more critical approach to the understanding of the biblical text. Specifically, Luther rejects Aquinas' understanding of a woman as a defective man – women and men are equal partners and, although it would be wrong to say that Luther can be seen to espouse the full equality of men and women as we might recognize these today, nevertheless his approach provides a major movement beyond Aquinas and a considerable step forward towards our present understanding of the equality of the two sexes.

The New Protestant Churches

Possibly the most significant development of the Reformation period was that individual Christians were given access to their own Bibles which, thanks to printing, were to be available to every adult who could read. The authority of the Bible rather than the authority of the Church became central. The equality of men and women was eventually realized by Protestants as they came to see the challenge of Christianity being to be obedient to God's will as found in the pages of the Bible. The practice of regular daily reading of the Bible increased and the most important unit within Christianity became the family. To be sure, the Church was also important, but the Church was recognized as being made up of individuals – although individual Protestant communities laid down firm rules which, if contravened, could result in ostracism.

Attitudes to sexuality did not necessarily become more liberal – in fact the Protestant Reformers, looking to St Augustine, treated sex with great suspicion. However, the attitude to having large families and to sexual relationships within the family became more positive, provided sex was intended for procreation. Marriage was seen as part of the divinely ordered plan and its purpose was the raising of children.

The idea that celibacy was a more holy life-style or was closer to God became, in Protestant Europe, a thing of the past. God could call people to his service either through a celibate or a married life-style, and the question for an individual was which of the two forms of life they were called to, since both were legitimate. In this respect, clergy and lay people were in the same position. The status of married women also changed in the Protestant Church, as there were no celibate religious orders which offered women a 'higher' spiritual route to God. The status of being a 'married woman' was therefore, by implication, raised as there was no higher status against which the married woman could be seen to be inferior. Having said this, the male still tended to be supreme. Roland Bainton describes the average household in the Reformation period as a place where 'the father was priest as well as magistrate, where family prayers and recital of catechism were daily exercises'.[8]

The Reformers often quoted the Letter to the Hebrews:

Let marriage be held in honour among all, and let the marriage bed be undefiled (Hebrews 13:4)

They also saw marriage as being blessed by God and even ordained by God because of the command in Genesis 1:28 that human beings should 'go out and multiply', and the fact that Jesus was brought up as part of a family was also seen as endorsing family life. However, it was clear to Protestants, as it had been to all their predecessors, that sexual desire went far beyond the purpose for which it was intended by God and they saw Augustine as providing the reason for this – namely the Fall (cf. p. 54). Lust and desire brought people to sin and this was due to disorder following the Fall. There was only one legitimate outlet for sexual activity and that was within marriage.

Summary

The Protestant Reformers did not bring about as radical a transformation as is sometimes supposed. In many ways they were

[8] Roland Bainton, *The Reformation of the Sixteenth Century*, Beacon Press, 1952, p. 255.

conservative and, going back to Augustine, retained most of his negative views on sex. Erasmus was more advanced and enlightened in his views than his supposed successors, but he was in a minority and, in the sexual sphere, the Reformation did not provide liberation or enlightenment – except insofar as it affirmed the role of women and the goodness of the married state.

Questions for Discussion

The Hebrew Scriptures and the Ten Commandments

1   What is the difference in the relationship between men and women in the two creation stories in the book of Genesis?

2   Are all or any of the ten commandments valid today? If some are valid but not all, then on what basis can some be given priority over others?

3   In the sexual arena, are there any absolute commands today originating in the Hebrew Scriptures which cannot have exceptions?

4   What were the main principles underlying the emphasis on the virginity of brides in the Hebrew Scriptures?

5   Do Old Testament references condemning homosexuality have any relevance today? What reasons would you give for your view?

6   What are the worst sins condemned in the Hebrew Scriptures?

7   In what ways were men and women treated differently in the field of sex, marriage and divorce in the Hebrew Scriptures with which you are familiar?

Jesus' Teachings and the Early Church

1   What are the teachings of Jesus about sexual ethics?

2   What were Jesus' teachings on divorce?

3 If you had to summarize the main part of Jesus' message, how would you do so and what significance do you consider this could have for marriage? Give your reasons.

4 How do St Paul's views on sex differ from those expressed by Jesus?

5 Why was Philo of Alexandria so influential in the development of ideas about sexuality?

6 Why did the early Christian Church come to attach so much importance to sexual ethics?

7 What are the key assumptions which explain why St Augustine considered that human sexuality originated in the Fall?

The Middle Ages and the Reformation

8 What are the key assumptions on which Natural Law rests? How can they be (a) rejected, or (b) supported?

9 Why is artificial birth control rejected by supporters of Natural Law?

10 What were the main differences between Protestants and Catholics in their views on sexual activity at the time of the Reformation?

11 Compare and contrast the approach of Orthodox and Catholic Christians to remarriage and divorce. Which position do you find more plausible and why?

12 Has a wife always got a duty to make herself sexually available to her husband? Justify your answer.

13 Why could it have been argued to be morally wrong for a man to make love to his wife if she was unable to have children?

14 Why did it take the Church so long to accept the possibility of marital rape?

PART 2

FINDING A NEW WAY FORWARD

NINE

Old Wine in New Bottles

The Basis for Present Sexual Ethics

There is no single view that can be described as 'the Christian view' on sexual ethics. There are, rather, a variety of radically different positions resting on different presuppositions. These include:

1 The first position, Catholic Natural Law, has been outlined in chapter 6. This is a deontological approach in that it arrives at certain absolute moral rules and sees acts as being good and bad in themselves irrespective of consequences. It is this approach that underlies documents such as the Roman Catholic document *Veritatis Splendor* which maintains that certain acts are 'intrinsically evil' irrespective of circumstances or consequences. This approach has its origins in the view that sexual activity has two purposes:

a) Procreation,
b) A remedy against sin

To which has more recently been added a third:

c) A unitive function

The Roman Catholic position traditionally emphasized (a) and (b), whereas today it emphasizes (a) and (c). It maintains that these two functions may not be separated. This refusal to separate two elements maintains the Aristotelian tradition that the purpose of sexual intercourse is primarily the production of children and, in the absence of at least the possibility of this, sees sex as primarily a selfish act. In *Humanae Vitae* (1968), the Catholic magisterium stated that 'each and every marriage act must remain open to the transmission of life', and more recently Pope John Paul II has declared that contraception is as grave a sin as abortion.

The Natural Law approach is based on an understanding of psychology and physiology which has long been shown to be flawed and thus can be seen to rest on foundations which are intellectually invalid. While it remains the basis of official Catholic teaching on sexual morality, many within the Church hold that Natural Law has never met human needs and that the present rules cannot be intellectually defended. Many Catholic scholars recognize it is not possible to stipulate that certain actions are 'intrinsically evil' if these actions are divorced entirely from their setting or intention. Joseph Fuchs, SJ, for example, maintains that what one *does* cannot, by itself, constitute the whole action. The act of placing the blade of a knife in a certain part of a person's body can be an attempt at healing, murder, self-defence or suicide.[1] The fact that it is not possible to foresee all the possible circumstances and intentions that could accompany any one particular action is enough to prevent the formulation of absolute rules. Fuch's position depends on the view that moral actions are crucially dependent on the intentions of the agent.

Another Catholic theologian, Richard McCormick, rejects Augustine's and Aquinas' view that lies represent a misuse of one's expressive powers (just as masturbation, sex without the possibility of conception, etc., represent the misuse of one's genitalia). He maintains that it is necessary to take into account a hierarchy of social values and to see, in the case of human speech, that its purpose is not simply to pass on correct information.[2] Similarly, the purpose of genitalia and sexuality is not simply, or even necessarily, procreation.

---

[1] Quoted in Bernard Hoose, *Proportionalism*, p. 35.
[2] Richard A. McCormick, *Notes on Moral Theology*, University Press of America, 1985.

2 The second alternative is to emphasize the 'unitive' function in sexuality ((c) above) as central in building love and to separate it from the procreative function. It is not for nothing that reference is made to 'making love' where two people who are committed to each other and deeply care for each other come together, but when it is necessarily linked (as the Roman Catholic Church maintains) with procreation, the unitive function withers into a secondary and derivative purpose.

The Church of England and the world-wide Episcopalian, Methodist and Reformed Churches have firmly put the unitive side of intercourse into central place. In the Church of England marriage service, three purposes are given for marriage:

- mutual support of husband and wife
- the unitive role of sex within marriage
- so that the couple 'may have children'

The wording of the second purpose is significant in conveying the positive role assigned to sexual intercourse:

It is given, that with delight and tenderness they may know each other in love, and, through the joy of their bodily union, may strengthen the union of their hearts and lives.

In today's complex world the Church of England's willingness to separate the unitive and procreative sides of sexual activity enjoys widespread acceptance. To maintain that the possibility or intention of procreation is a necessary condition for acceptable sexual activity within marriage may be a distortion based on errors made in the past – not least by Augustine and Aquinas.

3 The third alternative is a view which seeks to appeal directly to the Bible and maintains that the Bible lays down clear rules about sexual relationships which are as applicable today as at the time they were written. This book has made clear that, when modern biblical

scholarship is applied to the texts or simply when the texts are understood in their context, this approach fails. The texts are too culturally conditioned to be applied to today's problems without considerable interpretation.

4 The fourth approach is based on Situation Ethics which rejects any absolute moral rules and claims that Jesus came to call people into a love relationship with God and with one another.[3] What is morally right is that action which best promotes and furthers love. This is a consequentialist position in that it measures the rightness or wrongness of actions in terms of their consequences. Those who take this view will emphasize the unitive purpose of sexual relationships (and that they should necessarily involve 'making' or building love) and will maintain that human beings have been given the right, by God, to decide for themselves when procreation should take place, if at all. They would also reject the view that marriage should be regarded as a sexual outlet so that it provides a remedy against sin.

There are problems with this view as any idea of rules in the sexual realm is rejected and morality in this field becomes a matter for individual decision-making measured against the lofty Christian ideal of agapeistic or non-preferential love. It also does not take into account the effect of sexual activity on those involved and, to this extent, ignores the important part sexuality plays in our common human nature.

5 Certain Catholic theologians such as Bruno Schuller[4] and Bernard Hoose, have developed a new approach to Christian ethics – albeit one that is claimed to have deep roots in the Catholic tradition. This is called Proportionalism and it maintains that there are certain firm, general rules to guide human conduct and, in most situations, these rules will apply. However, in specific and unusual situations there may be a proportionate

[3] Put forward in systematic form by Joseph Fletcher in *Situation Ethics*, SCM Press, 1966.

[4] Bruno Schuller, 'Various Types of Grounding for Moral Norms', *Readings* 1:187–8.

reason which can justify breaking the rule and this is then the morally right thing to do. For instance, there may be a general rule that adultery is wrong but, in a prison camp situation, a woman may sleep with a guard in order to feed her starving children or to secure their release and this would be a morally right action. In Just War thinking, the idea of Proportionalism is fundamental both in demanding a proportionate response to aggression and demanding that the way war is fought must be proportionate to the ill suffered. Proportionalism has however been strongly condemned by Pope John Paul II and the Catholic magisterium because it departs from the absolute basis of Natural Law and allows exceptions to supposed firm rules. Nevertheless, many Catholics have found this position persuasive. It allows one to maintain the claim that there are general moral rules but to accommodate the intuition that in some rare cases exceptions must be made. In fact, this is a position that Aquinas might well have endorsed, as he maintained that whilst there are certain 'primary precepts' which always apply in the moral arena, at the more detailed level of 'secondary precepts', moral rules may be subject to rare exceptions.[5]

Proportionalism is a persuasive and important position, but it may be argued that it fails in the area of sexual ethics. It fails not because firm rules may not have exceptions in particular circumstances but because there are no clear grounds for firm rules in the sexual arena from which there may be exceptions. The first part of this book has made the difficulties of arriving at such firm rules clear, and it is necessary to distinguish between the tradition which has passed down what appears to be firm rules and, on the other hand, firm rules which can legitimately claim intellectual or biblical foundations.

Some Proportionalists maintain that there are no firm rules from which there can be exceptions – instead they seek for the fundamental nature of human beings and see moral guidance being

---

[5] Aquinas, cf *The Puzzle of Ethics*, Peter Vardy and Paul Grosch.

framed by reference to this understanding. This approach is similar to the one which will be argued for in this book.

None of the above approaches, except perhaps a version of the last, are adequate to act as a foundation for sexual morality today. What is more, none of them adequately take into account the erotic element in some human relationships. Nowhere is this element better portrayed than in the Song of Songs.

The Song of Songs

The Song of Songs is an uncomfortable book to find in the Bible. Its erotic imagery is very direct and is at variance with what most theologians and the Church have regarded as the 'appropriate' attitude to sex. For centuries, therefore, the attempt was made to explain it as an allegory and to reject the idea that it was literally a series of passionate love poems. Most biblical scholars, however, reject the allegorical interpretation which does violence to the text and is exceptionally hard to justify. If one concentrates on the text itself (as anyone who wants to take the Bible seriously should do), then there is nothing within the book or outside it to suggest that it should be taken at other than face value. This may be uncomfortable to those who approach the book with prejudice (meaning, literally, having 'prejudged' their views beforehand). However, it is necessary to recognize that this book which is universally acknowledged as part of the Bible is full of the most explicit sexual verses which glory in the wonder, the joy and the beauty of a man and a woman making love.

The book does not describe the love of a single man and a single woman – it is a love poem which can be applied to any couple in any age and any place. It moves from the man talking to the woman to the woman talking to the man – their passion for each other is equal and they long for the joy of the other's embrace. The images are clear and, to the prudish, uncomfortable. The first verses start with the woman speaking to the man:

'O that you would kiss me with the kisses of your mouth!
For your love is better than wine ...
Draw me after you, let us make haste ...' (Song of Songs 1:2,4)

The poem alternates between the man and the woman speaking, the following verses are among those attributed to the man:

Behold you are beautiful, my love;
   behold you are beautiful;
     your eyes are doves.
Behold you are beautiful, my beloved,
   truly lovely ...(1:15)

Your teeth are like a flock of shorn ewes
   that have come up from washing,
Your two breasts are like two fawns,
   twins of a gazelle
    that feed among the lilies ...
you have ravished my heart with
   a glance of your eyes ... (4:2,5,9)

How fair and pleasant you are,
   O loved one, delectable maiden!
You are stately as a palm tree
   and your breasts are like its clusters.
I say I will climb the palm tree
   and lay hold of the branches.
Oh, may your breasts be like clusters of the vine,
   and the scent of your breath like apples,
and your kisses like the best wine
   that goes down smoothly ... (7:6–9)

The Song of Songs is a poem which glories in the physical love of two individuals, but it also operates at a much more profound level as well. There is physical desire and the urge for intimacy and the joy of the kisses and embraces of the other, but these express something of incredible depth. It is, truly, a love song. It is sometimes difficult for us in the modern age, when sex has become a commodity, to capture the innocence of real love of which physical closeness should be the expression, but the Song of Songs does just this. The woman in the Song goes to bed alone and the poem tells of her dream. She readies herself for her beloved, who is knocking at the door of her heart. She imagines herself with no clothes on:

> I had put off my garment,
> > how could I put it on? (5:3)

but she falls asleep and does not hear her beloved come to her door. She rushes to open it, but it is too late and he has gone. In her dream, she rushes out into the street searching for him, only to be beaten by the watchmen who take away the cloak she had put on. She cries out to the other women (the daughters of Jerusalem):

> I adjure you, O daughters of Jerusalem,
> > if you find my beloved,
> that you tell him
> > I am sick with love. (5:8)

They, however, are more cynical and say that the man she seeks is just another man, there are plenty of others and he is no different: 'What is your beloved more than another beloved?' they ask (5:9). This gives the occasion for the woman to go into a hymn of praise about the beauty and virtue of her beloved – she talks of his lips, his cheeks, his arms, his body, his legs, his appearance and his speech. She ends as follows:

> His speech is sweet,
> > and he is altogether desirable.
> This is my beloved and this is my friend,
> > O daughters of Jerusalem. (5:16)

'This is my beloved and this is my friend' – with this ringing declaration the woman expresses not only her love and commitment but the depth of their relationship. Her beloved is not any man whom she finds desirable – he is her friend. This speaks of an intimacy and a sharing, an engagement that goes beyond and yet is expressed by physical closeness. Certainly, there is intimate friendship manifested as erotic passion at work, but the passion arises out of a deep love, understanding and commitment to the other. The love is entirely mutual, the love of two equals:

'I am my beloved's and my beloved is mine ...' (6:3)

We have here no idea of female subservience to the male, but two equal human beings who have found true love. This love is not a momentary emotion but a yearning for and commitment to the other which will endure through the years:

Set me as a seal upon your heart,
    as a seal upon your arm;
for love is strong as death,
    jealousy is cruel as the grave.
Its flashes are flashes of fire,
    a most vehement flame.
Many waters cannot quench love,
    neither can floods drown it.
If a man offered for love
    all the wealth of his house
    it would be utterly scorned. (8:6–7)

The woman in Israel's households was of great importance and, in particular, was seen as the bringer of peace to the home. The Hebrew concept of peace – *shalom* – represents a profound sense of well-being, happiness and contentment which ideally should be found in the home. The woman was traditionally seen as the bringer of this. The Song of Songs recognizes this when the woman says: 'I was in his eyes as one who brings peace' (8:10).

In a way, this peace is the culmination of a love and trust which, though given passionate physical expression, goes far beyond this. Peace is the fruit of love and of passion when the latter is a genuine expression of deep affection and commitment.

Part of the tremendous strength of the faith of the people of Israel was that it was life-affirming rather than life-denying. Christian faith is said to be 'incarnational' in that it is not 'other wordly' – God has come to earth as a human being and the old divide between heaven and earth has been done away with. God can be found in the normal day-to-day activities of life. Yet this Christian insight arose out of a Jewish understanding that was broadly similar. Human love is a pointer to God's love and is, essentially, good. All too often Christian writers have denied that sexual love is good. In Hebrew, the same word is used for human love as is used for love of God – and this is significant. God created men and women as equals, as gendered beings, and the love they have for each other is a reflection of the love of God.

It is not only the Song of Songs that produces flashes of a positive understanding of human sexuality. Many Christian mystics such as Julian of Norwich (1343–1423) speak of human love positively:

> I understand that our sensuality is founded in nature, in mercy, and in grace, and this foundation enables us to receive gifts which lead us to endless life. For I saw very clearly that our substance is in God, and I also saw that God is in our sensuality, for in the same instant and place in which our soul is made sensual, in that same instant and place exists the city of God, ordained for him from without beginning.

However, such passages are rare, and it is at least possible that this may be due to the paucity of feminine writers in Christian history. The male perspective has dominated and, with it, a suspicion of tenderness, gentleness, compassion and love, as well as the importance of human relationships. These essential ingredients of what it is to be human can no longer be neglected.

Summary

The Anglican Church has a strong commitment to a 'fearless love of truth', as the Declaration of the 1930 Lambeth Conference states, and St Thomas Aquinas also sought truth. This search for a truthful understanding in the sexual field has never been more urgent than today. The time has come for a re-evaluation of human sexual morality – yet it is difficult to know where to begin such a re-evaluation as so much of the ground seems uncertain. None of the approaches set out in the first part of this chapter fit easily into the approach taken by the Song of Songs. The love portrayed in the Song of Songs may, indeed, give access to God and to another dimension of reality. The centrality of love is emphasized by Jesus, by St Paul, by John the Evangelist (particularly in the First Epistle), by St Francis, St Catherine of Sienna, Martin Luther King and Mother Teresa. The Franciscan tradition of theology has always been dominated by love unlike the Dominican tradition of St Thomas Aquinas which was dominated by reason and which has led to much of the present negative attitude to sexual activity.

Kelsey and Kelsey put the problem like this:

> Love ... is a very mysterious force, and one with strange consequences. But the Western Church has more or less forgotten about the importance of the strange and mysterious; for several centuries now it has had its thinking determined, not by the Platonic understanding, but by the rationalism of Aristotle and Descartes, and their emphasis on reason and the mind. Consequently the Church has become almost antagonistic to the irrational aspects of religious experience. Those who speak in tongues, have visions, and dream dreams come in for a rejection comparable to that inflicted upon people with homosexual inclinations. Where reason is enthroned as ultimate, all the divine madness – all the non-rational religious encounters that

are so central to the thinking of Plato and so foreign to that of Aristotle – are inevitably devalued, love included.[6]

Talk of love, however, is very vague, and greater precision is required. In the remainder of this book an attempt will be made to outline a new approach to sexual ethics which draws on the past as well as on our current knowledge about human beings. First, however, it is important to understand something of the insights of psychology regarding human sexual development.

[6] Morton T. Kelsey & Barbara Kelsey, *Sacrament of Sexuality*, Element Books, 1991, pp. 201–2.

TEN

Psychological Perspectives

Freudian Theory

If one is to understand the role of sex in a person's life today it is important to have some understanding of psychological insights. Freudian psychology is one particularly useful and instructive way of attempting to understand human experience and behaviour although, however influential and helpful it may have been and still remains, it must be accepted that it is one way amongst others.

Sigmund Freud (1856–1939) considered that a human being's personality is primarily determined by two basic instincts – sexuality and aggression – and the key issue is how the individual comes to terms with these. The opening paragraph of Freud's *Three Essays of the Theory of Sexuality* is as follows:

> Popular opinion has quite definite ideas about the nature and characteristics of the sexual instinct. It is generally understood to be absent in childhood, to set in at the time of puberty in connection with the process of coming to maturity and to be revealed in the manifestation of an irresistible attraction exercised by one sex upon the other; while its aim is presumed to be sexual union, or at all events action leading in that direction. We have every reason to believe, however, that these views give a very false picture of the true situation. If we look into them more closely we shall find that they contain a number of errors, inaccuracies and hasty conclusions.[1]

[1] Volume 7 of *The Standard Edition of the Complete Psychological Works of Sigmund Freud*, ed. James Strachey et al., 24 vols, Hogarth Press & Institute of Psychoanalysis, 1953–74.

Freud's methodology did not start with assumptions about the 'normality' of heterosexual attraction, instead he studied what he saw as the facts. In this, at least, his methodology was similar to that of Aristotle who also sought to work from 'the facts' of human nature. It was clear to Freud that sexual attraction was a very powerful force but, in different people, it could be directed in many different directions. A man might be sexually attracted to a woman, to another man, to young boys around puberty, to young boys well under the age of puberty, to young girls, to girls around the age of puberty or various apparent substitutes such as bondage; leather; punishment or even an animal. Similarly, women may be attracted to as wide a range of overlapping and alternative possibilities. Instead of regarding these as aberrations, Freud considered they had to be taken into account in any successful theory of human psychology.

In *The Interpretation of Dreams* (1900), Freud saw the human psyche as much more complex than had previously been imagined. He maintained that the human psyche was the battleground of three mechanisms or forces:

1 **The id** – this represents the basic biological drives which demand instant satisfaction. Freud saw all these drives as being fundamentally sexual in origin, although his definition of 'sexual' goes beyond the genital/physiological to include both the affective and social dimensions of human relationships. Freud considered the id to be entirely amoral and, if left uncontrolled, it would seek pleasure in any circumstances. It is the blind, pleasure-seeking force of the universe.

2 **The superego** – the internalized perceived demands and expectation from 'parents' (whoever may be doing or have done the parenting) which preconsciously censors anything which might threaten the person's acceptability to those to whom he or she is, as an infant, utterly dependent. The superego represses unpleasant memories particularly those which are associated with negative

sexual experiences or perceptions. The superego can be seen as a censor which keeps us from remembering fantasies, negative experiences or even dreams which express our sexual nature. These are censored so that their sexual connotations are removed.

3 **The ego** – the conscious, self-aware self which is able to take account of reality. The ego is the ringmaster which tries to balance external reality and the largely unconscious forces of the id and the superego.

The workings of the id and the superego are outside the realm of conscious awareness. Human beings, according to Freud, typically repress memories, fantasies, dreams and other influences which cause pain or anxiety. All the tangled sexual impressions of early childhood (for instance, in the case of boys, oedipal complexes, hatred of the father as a sexual competitor, desire for the mother, etc.) get firmly repressed by the time the child reaches seven years of age. After this, these repressed memories will work in the sub-conscious but the growing adolescent or the mature adult may be completely unaware that they exist.

The aim of the id, for Freud, is to maximize pleasure – the superego only affects this by introducing the calculation of what is acceptable and what is compatible with the maximization of plea-sure. Some pleasures desired by the id may, according to the prudent calculations of the superego, be more likely to be realized or to be maximized if they are postponed. However, both id and superego work together in the service of the pleasure principle – the one acting as the fundamental drive and the other as the driver which steers and controls. Their objectives are the same.

Freud saw the task of psychoanalysis as being to bring the individual into an awareness of these three instinctive forces so that they could be integrated and human beings could exercise some control over their lives. Freud considered that the drive stemming from libido (the energy emanating from the id) can be associated with three distinct parts of the body which correspond to three stages:

The Oral Phase

This develops in the earliest months of a human life when the baby is stimulated most by sucking on the mother's breast or on substitutes such as a dummy or a towel. The crucial part of this stage is stimulation of the mouth and includes sucking, swallowing and eating all of which give sexual satisfaction – it includes being cuddled and fed by the mother and the fixation is on the mother figure as the source of gratification.

The Anal Phase

After the first year, the focus in a normally developing child switches from the mouth as an organ of pleasure to the anus for the second and third years of life, with an emphasis on being able to control excretions and being praised for doing so.

The Phallic Phase

Finally, in the fourth and fifth years attention switches to the genitalia. It is from this stage that Freud produced his famous oedipal theory. The name stems from the Greek tragic play *Oedipus*, in which a young man unknowingly falls in love with and makes love to his mother. Freud considers that the four- to five-year-old male feels a genital attraction to his mother, but he is subconsciously aware that this brings him into conflict with his father. He therefore suppresses this feeling because he is nervous of what he perceives as the threat of castration as the possible punishment by the father who may see his desire as an attempt to take the mother away. The young boy therefore suppresses these feelings and identifies instead with his father (an early example of 'if you can't beat them, join them!') and it is this identification that establishes his masculinity. A similar process is followed for a girl child – although Freud stressed the male anatomy as being more important than the female.

Freud maintains that an individual's essential sexual orientation is established by the age of five or six. This may remain latent until puberty, but after puberty is reached the sexual organs develop and these may, or may not, be used to express the orientation that has been established. However, he takes little or no account of the environment in which children grow up and it has been demonstrated that the gender role assigned to the child by parents can have a major and decisive influence in establishing adult sexual orientation. A father may treat a young girl as if she was a boy, may dress her as a boy and give her solely male role models to whom to relate. Such influences can confuse the sexual identity created for the child and this can manifest itself in similar confusion in later life.

Freud maintained that sexuality sometimes becomes merged into power and violence. In *Civilization and its Discontents* he argues that the less violence is involved in sexuality, the more sexuality comes close to its real meaning. Sexual relationships can be seen as extending from a mutual, loving relationship to rape at the other extreme. Rape is the violent subjugation of one party (either a woman or a man) to the demands and wishes of another without her or his consent. This, clearly, is morally evil and a denial of the autonomy of the other party – yet it is distressingly frequent. Rape in prison, in conditions of slavery, on the streets of large cities or even within marriage is far too common and all too often sex involves the exercise of power. Any ethical understanding of sexual behaviour has to take a firm stand in rejecting this and showing its devastating effect both on the victim and, in human terms, on the perpetrator.

Perhaps Freud's most important claims are that adult sexuality is determined within the first five years of a child's life and his stress on the central importance of biology or genitalia in establishing sexual patterns. Freud's ideas have deeply influenced Western thinking about sexual development, yet they may well be mistaken. In particular, the power of the id as the fundamental force underlying all human actions may overstate the influence of human sexuality. His account also takes no account of God or of human moral autonomy. Freud's analysis is also heavily masculine oriented – he has a very limited view of female sexuality. Freud does, however, recognize that there is a key transition in human development from seeking pleasure to responding to reality – instead of simply demanding that our needs for pleasure be satisfied, the developing adult can order and control these desires. However, this is only possible if development is not stunted. If, for instance, one or other parent is missing or love is denied to the child, then the child may become locked into an emotional insecurity in which key parts of his or her humanity are denied because they have never been sufficiently affirmed. If sexual expression is condemned or treated as 'dirty' or unacceptable this may distort the whole of an individual's personality.

Abraham Maslow says:

> Freud's greatest discovery is that the great cause of much psychological illness is the fear of knowledge of oneself – of one's emotions, impulses, memories, capacities, potentialities and one's destiny. (As Freud said) 'To be completely honest with oneself is the very best effort a human being can make.'[2]

The Parent/Child Relationship

Erik Erikson builds on Freud's work and, in particular, agrees with Freud's stress on the importance of human psychological growth in early childhood. In the first year of life he sees trust developing in an unfolding process that will continue in future years. This trust in parents can, Erikson maintains, be mirrored in trust in God in later life – someone who cannot develop a sense of parental trust may have great difficulty trusting God. In the second and third years, he considers that human autonomy as well as shame and doubt emerge as the child becomes conscious of itself as a being separate from its mother. The child develops a range of skills from walking to feeding and toilet training which enables it to operate on its own, but it also learns about failure and mistakes. In the fourth and fifth years, initiative emerges as the child takes responsibility for its own actions, and Erikson links this sense of initiative with a developing idea of guilt for the child's own failures. Parents are vital at this stage

[2] Abraham Maslow, *Toward a Psychology of Being*, p. 57.

(as in all the other stages) by helping the child to rectify mistakes and to develop confidence in its own abilities. If parental love is absent, the child will increasingly blame itself for its mistakes and even its human need for love will not be able to be accepted and will be seen by the child as being selfish and wrong.

Despair is one of the most terrible emotions a human being can feel and yet it is surprisingly common. It can lead an individual into a downward cycle of depression, but it can also, if properly handled, be an opportunity to come to terms with the past and to grow as a human being. There may be many reasons for despair, but they can certainly include the despair that comes from being unable to accept or to give love. Modern psychology has shown clearly that the antecedents of this may well lie in problems in childhood when parents fail to express love, fail to accept love and fail to show love no matter what the child does. As Jack Dominian says:

> We cannot earn or buy love from others; we can only receive it and accept it on the basis that, having first been loved by our parents for simply being ourselves, we continue to be loved by others on the same basis.[3]

However, when parents do not love children 'for simply being themselves', when their love is either non-existent, judgmental or conditional, then the child may grow into an adult who simply cannot relate to others or to him or herself.

Jung – Psychology and Spirituality

The great counter to Freud's ideas comes in the work of Carl Jung (1875–1961). It was Jung's rejection of Freud's view that sexuality was the single most important influence on humans that led to his breaking from Freud. Jung agreed with Freud that sexuality as well as greed, selfishness and aggression were key motivating factors in human

[3] Jack Dominian, *Cycles of Affirmation*, DLT, 1975.

behaviour – however, he also maintained that humans had a drive towards integration and wholeness. Unlike Freud, Jung did not straightforwardly reject belief in God and maintained that sexuality was a powerful way of integrating the personality by way of integrating opposites. He also saw sex as a symbol of the encounter between the human being and God (although what Jung means by 'God' is debatable and Jung cannot be taken to refer directly to the God of Christian theology). The way to eliminate mental sickness is to try to bring the individual into touch with the divine in a real and profound way.

Jung considered that women contained an aspect of the divine and that men were incapable of coming to wholeness without relating to the feminine principle. Deep in the human psyche there was a feminine primal aspect which Jung termed the anima. In his final work, *Answer to Job* (which is widely regarded as semi-autobiographical), Jung sees himself on the side of Job in his protest against God but also sees himself supported by God's feminine side represented by Wisdom or Mary. Jung was deeply impressed by the Catholic dogma of the Assumption of the Virgin Mary into Heaven and saw this as a way of integrating the feminine into an otherwise male deity – the feminine was placed alongside the 'male' Trinity. There are parallels here with the ying and yang principle of Chinese philosophy, in which the two aspects are intertwined and human wholeness is fostered by maintaining the two in balance.

Women who do not come to terms with their masculine aspect or men who do not come into contact with their feminine side will fail to come to wholeness. As William Kraft puts it:

> Within every man there is a woman, and within every woman there is a man. Although the sexes are distinct, they are not separate. A phenomenology of sexual encounters indicates that a man and a woman experience something familiar and something foreign in each other – that one sex is the complement of the other. In Jungian terms, a man meets his hidden anima or a woman her animus in the other sex ...[4]

---

[4] William Kraft, *Sexual Dimensions of the Celibate Life*, 1979, p. 36.

In other words, no man or woman is complete. Jung can be seen as affirming the Genesis text which points to the unity of male and female – human beings need to come to wholeness in recognizing their incompleteness and their need for relationship with their counterpart. This can only happen, Jung maintains, when women and men are in open, equal relationships. If this does not happen, the necessary integration is difficult if not impossible to achieve. One possible consequence of this is that, say, a man who is very open to the female side of his personality may be particularly well integrated. He may have:

> ... a great capacity for friendship which often creates ties of astonishing tenderness between men and may even rescue friendships between the sexes from the limbo of the impossible. He may have good taste and an aesthetic sense which are fostered by the presence of a feminine streak. Then he may be supremely gifted as a teacher because of his almost feminine insight and tact. He is likely to have a feeling for history, and to be conservative in the best sense and cherish the value of the past. Often he is endowed with a wealth of religious feelings ... and a spiritual sensitivity which makes him responsive to revelation.[5]

There are strong echoes here of the Genesis creation story which sees men and women as being created from the unified *adam* or earth creature (cf. p. 5ff.) – neither a man nor a woman is whole until they can integrate both the male and female aspects of their personality.

Jung was concerned with that rare person who was committed to becoming fully themselves, to becoming a complete and integrated human being. This involved, he considered, a process of 'individuation' in which the conscious and unconscious sides of the psyche are brought together. However, unlike Freud, Jung

[5] Carl Gustav Jung, *The Collected Works of C. G. Jung*, trans. R. F. C. Hull, vol. 9, p. 71.

maintains that humans share a collective unconscious which lies deep within the psyche and which is derived from the past history of human beings and which also needs to be integrated in the search for selfhood. Within this collective unconscious exist primal images or archetypes, and one of these archetypes may be a symbolic reference for God. Whether there exists a God beyond the archetype is not always clear in Jung's writings. Initially he shared Freud's view that God was a human projection but he later came to at least appear to be open to the possibility that the archetype was an 'imprint' of God.

An alternative psychological approach which has grown out of classic psychoanalysis is called object-relations theory. This holds that, from the moment of birth our primary drive is towards relationships. All human beings have a relation with their parent or parents which combines instinct and love. We learn to feel wanted, recognized and loved in our relationships with our parents or we can feel unwanted, neglected and unappreciated. These experiences shape our future understanding of sexuality. As Dominion puts it:

> When we make love as adults we are reacting to more than a body; we are responding to a person. How we respond to that person depends on how we experienced our parents and ourselves as children ... If we were neglected as children it is easy to feel that the person who is making love to us only wants our body and does not love us as a person. The way we were treated as children makes an enormous difference to how we interact in sexual intercourse because we relive with the person with whom we are making love the most intimate experience of childhood.[6]

The relation between psychological states and spiritual insights and experiences has been much discussed in modern studies in psychology of religion. Mary Anne Oliver's book *Conjugal Spirituality* is a sustained attempt to bring together sexuality and spirituality and to see the two as complementary rather than

[6] Jack Dominion, *God, Sex and Love*, SCM Press, 1984, p. 24.

112

opposed. This represents a marked change from the views of Augustine and Aquinas, continued through the Middle Ages, which saw 'the way of God' as being opposed to all forms of sexual activity and associated sex with a disorder of the will which required suppression and repression.

Few Churches today have taken these new insights on board – with the result that moral rules in the sexual field tend to have ignored the findings of psychology and to hold onto insights which have been shown to be intellectually flawed. Donald Goergan wrote on this theme in 1974:

> The dichotomy between sexuality and spirituality and between spirituality and marriage is destructive and inappropriate. Integration lies in seeing how we can be both sexual and spiritual simultaneously and in seeing that choosing one way of life does not imply the inferiority of the other.[7]

Development and Wholeness

Freud's emphasis on the importance of childhood in our sexual development has been amply confirmed by psychologists over the last thirty years who have seen that many personality problems and problems with sexuality that arise in adolescence and in later life stem from childhood experiences. The importance of these elements is clear, but so is the importance of integration emphasized by the Jungian school.

Some of the worst cases of arrested sexual development occur with sexual abuse where a young girl or boy is physically abused by an adult who may be a man or woman, mother or father, relative or stranger. Abuse can range from an adult gently 'playing with' the child's genitalia to violent intercourse at a very early age and extend to someone in a position of power (teacher, priest, doctor) using this position to impose their own sexual will on someone in their

[7] Donald Georgan, *The Sexual Celibate*, p. 12.

charge. Such abuse leaves a long shadow over the developing adult who may both see themselves partly to blame (particularly if, as can sometimes happen, feelings of pleasure may be associated with the abuse, leading the child to feel partly responsible – however ludicrous this may seem to others). They may also feel 'used' and therefore associate all future forms of sexual relationship with dominance and abuse.

Even though the evidence is now clear that sexual abuse is far more common than has ever been accepted in the past, it is still a relatively small minority who will be scarred in this way. Many others, however, may be deeply affected and psychologically damaged by the negative images given out about sexuality by parents and others. For instance:

- A baby may be smacked for 'playing with itself' even though it is now recognized that this is a normal part of child development.
- The toddler may be taught the names of different parts of the body, but the penis or vagina may never be named as these are considered 'dirty' and must never be referred to.
- The child may never see his or her parents naked, embracing passionately or even kissing.
- Parents may never talk about sex and, when a couple are seen making love on the television, however tenderly, may quickly switch channels or regard this as 'unsuitable'.
- The young adolescent may never be able to talk about his or her sexual development, periods, erections or the like with parents or even with trusted teachers – thus giving the impression that these are 'taboo' subjects instead of something normal and good.
- Masturbation, which almost every young adult male and the majority of young adult females practice, may be described as 'wicked', 'evil' and parents and others may even try to shock young people to stop them doing this (for instance previous generations of boys were told that masturbation made you blind).
- A child may come across a pornographic magazine and, instead

of being encouraged to see this as something debasing to women, may be punished by their parents for looking at it at all. They may feel that they even have to hide the fact that they have seen it – again confirming them in their view that anything to do with sex is 'dirty' and preventing them from distinguishing between 'making love' as part of a deep, loving relationship and something crude and dehumanizing.

All these and other events may cause the child and the young adult to have a profoundly negative view of sex – instead of seeing it as something good, the young adult can see it as something negative, even evil. If this happens, the developing adult becomes 'stuck' and does not develop into full adulthood and maturity. Many people may be stuck in a childhood stage of sexual development. Physically they may be completely mature and 'normal', but psychologically and emotionally they have not developed beyond some early childhood stage. In this case, psychological help or counselling may well be necessary to help the individual come to terms with their background and to seek release from it. This can be a very painful process and many people are unwilling to embark on the path that leads to maturity precisely because they find the path too painful and are unwilling to unlock old, perhaps deeply buried and almost certainly painful memories. Yet this process of 'unlocking' may well be essential if wholeness and full development into healthy adulthood and a mature understanding of human personhood is to occur.

Central to psychological understandings of human personhood is the notion that the part of human beings about which most of us are consciously aware is, like the tip of an iceberg, the part above the surface of the sea. However, lurking beneath are forces, drives and repressed memories which have a vital effect on who we are. It is in coming to understand the whole iceberg and to integrate its different parts that a human being can come to full humanity.

Jesus forgave people their sins before he healed them[8] – this may

---

[8] Cf., for example, Mark 2:1–12.

seem strange today but it shows deep psychological understanding. Adults have to come to terms with their past failures or what they see as their past failures if they are to come to wholeness. They have to come to accept themselves and see that they are loved by God whatever they have done. Indeed, if one is a Christian, this may be the most radical part of the Christian message – that God loves those who have failed, those who are not whole. It may indeed be that the path to full humanity lies through first recognizing that each of us is, in some way or another, broken.

To summarize, the first of four fundamental principles governing sexual morality today can now be put forward:

> Psychology has made clear the intimate link between sexuality, personality and human development as well as the need for human integration. Sexuality is an essential part of human nature and each person has to come to wholeness by being able to accept and balance the different aspects of their nature. Sexuality and spirituality may be seen to be connected. The ability to love and to accept love, to form relationships and to enter into mature, adult sexual bonds depend to a larger extent on the experiences one has as a young child. Early experiences can distort the development process and can cause adults to be psychologically immature. The impact of parents and a warm, stable, loving home environment is important to psychological well-being. If these are absent, distortions are likely to result which may not be resolvable without help later in life. The negative view of human sexual nature deriving from the Christian tradition needs to be rejected and a positive approach taken to the wholeness of human experience in giving and receiving love.

ELEVEN

A New Way Forward

Any new approach to sexual ethics must take seriously the tradition from the past and the accumulated wisdom of previous experience and yet recognize present realities. These realities include the recognition of women as autonomous individuals; the insights of psychology; the improved understanding of the cultural relativity of much traditional thinking on sexual matters and the depth, complexity and profundity of relationships between human beings.

The rationality of the two positions underlying Aquinas and Aristotle's views have much merit — namely:

a) That there are truths to be sought in the moral arena and that personal intuition or conscience alone are unreliable guides. We may never be able to fully arrive at the truth about what it is to be human but, over time, our knowledge should develop and progress as it does in every other field — and this will affect any sound understanding of morality, and

b) That human beings share a common human nature.

Aquinas was an intellectual genius with profound insights into many areas of theology and philosophy — he worked with the latest understandings available at his time and had a passionate concern for truth. Any modern approach to sexual ethics should share the same aims.

The Roman Catholic Church still bases its sexual morality on Aquinas and Aristotle even though, as this book has made clear, their conclusions may well be flawed. As the Catholic psychiatrist

Jack Dominian puts it (referring to the 1968 document *Humanae Vitae*, though the same point could just as readily refer to later Catholic documents such as the 1993 statement on ethics, *Veritatis Splendor*):

> In referring to *Humanae Vitae* it is vital to remind ourselves that this remains the official teaching of the Roman Catholic Church. The fact is that the overwhelming majority of Roman Catholic moral theologians and the faithful have rejected this teaching and there is a continuous tension between the teaching authority and the rest of the Roman Catholic community. The essence of the teaching depends on the view that there is an essential link between sexual intercourse and procreation which must not be denied. At the heart of this view is an instinctual, biological view of sexual intercourse which ... is inconsistent with reality.[1]

However, although Aquinas' conclusions may be rejected, his methodology need not be and it has still much to teach us. Aquinas considered that, by examining human beings, we could establish the *telos* or purpose of human existence. In other words, Aquinas was attempting to 'start with the facts' of human nature, and this seems a logical and sensible way of proceeding. If one wants to determine what it is to be a good fox or flea, then one needs to study foxes and fleas to understand what their individual natures are. The same, it may be argued, applies to human beings. However, if one is going to do this one has to take account of the latest understanding of physiology and psychology. If this is accepted, then it would amount to endorsement of Aquinas' methodology but bringing it up to date with the latest understandings of human nature. Such an approach, it can be argued, is faithful to that of Aquinas.

[1] Jack Dominion & Hugh Montefiore, *God, Sex and Love*, SCM Press, 1989, p. 25.

The Lessons of Physiology and Psychology

1   Human bodies are complex and, unlike that of all other mammals, human sexuality is not necessarily related to conception. In all other mammals it is clear when the female is fertile, generally by some discharge which gives off a scent which is attractive to males. Although human females may have a slight discharge at certain times of the month, there are no outward signs detectable by a man that a woman is fertile. This strongly implies that sexuality has purposes other than reproduction. As Jared Diamond puts it:

> In these days of growing human overpopulation, one of the most paradoxical tragedies, in my view, is the Roman Catholic Church's insistence that copulation has conception as its only natural purpose, and that the rhythm method is the only proper means of birth control. These claims would be valid for gorillas and most other mammals, but not for us. In no other species besides man has the purpose of copulation become so unrelated to conception, or the rhythm method so unsuited for contraception.[2]

Unlike other animals, human beings are sexual creatures at all times and not just at times determined by the female cycle. This opens up the possibility for the right or wrong use of sexual behaviour in a way that does not apply in the animal kingdom. A person who abandons him or herself to the basest physical desires is sometimes described as having an 'animal' nature, but this does a great disservice to the animal world where such behaviour does not occur. Someone who behaves like this is certainly a human being, and is using his or her humanity in a depraved, not to say 'evil' way that will damage him or herself as well as others. There are no parallels in the animal world.

[2] Jared Diamond, 'Everything else you wanted to know about sex, but that you'd never ask,' *Discover*, April 1985, pp. 73–4.

2   As we learn more about human bodies, we now know that the human male produces large quantities of sperm and, in a young man, these are released. If they are not released by normal sexual activity or masturbation then this will occur in the night as a matter of normal physiology, and this will often be accompanied by dreams. Past generations have seen these 'nocturnal emissions' as sinful and they have been a cause of guilt and anxiety for countless numbers of people through the Middle Ages and beyond. We now recognize that they are a normal part of sexual development.

3   Female sexuality is now recognized as being complex with a woman's body responding to stimuli in various different parts including general caresses, kisses and also breast stimulation. Both vaginal and clitoral stimulation can also produce orgasms of different types and of different intensity. Different women will react differently to sexual activity – in some orgasms may be rare and difficult, in others they may occur very readily. In the past, sexual activity has been defined predominantly in male terms and, for instance, the Church's definition of adultery depends on defining adultery as penetration by the male – this has failed to take into account the complexity and sophistication of the female sexual response. Sound thinking about morality, if it aims to start from the facts of human nature (as Aquinas claimed it should), needs to take such factors into account.

4   Biologically, there is a great deal in common between all human beings – they share a DNA which, by and large, is nearly identical (although the variations are significant for individuals) and their physiologies are similar. As an example, a leading pharmacist in Britain now produces a battery-powered device which can be used by any woman in the world between 14 and 45+ which will tell them, by means of red or green lights, whether or not they are fertile and thus likely to conceive (there is a third, yellow light which indicates an uncertain reading and which requires a further urine test). There could be no better evidence of the commonalty of human beings, since this test will work on any woman no matter what their race or origin.

5   Masters and Johnson in *The Pleasure Bond* argue that sexual satisfaction is as much psychological as physical and that sexual relations are a form of communication that only reaches its full potential if it expresses a depth of commitment that extends to other areas of the individuals' lives.[3] Touch is vital and caresses and tenderness have a central role to play. The centrality of relationships between human beings both in friendship and in marriage has not been sufficiently taken into account by previous generations of theologians and moral philosophers, and any approach to sexual ethics today must take this seriously.

6   Sexual activity partly results in a release of tension which can be positive and beneficial, even though casual sex can be damaging and undermining of the identity and worth of human beings (see below). A denial of all sexual activity can cause damage and negative effects on the whole personality – effects which may often demand release in other, negative areas including paedophilia, violence, alcoholism and depression. Physical closeness and intimate love may well encourage a person to understand gentleness, tenderness and care for another in a way that he or she had never before understood.

7   As was made clear in the previous chapter, the work of psychologists has taught us much about the essential part human sexuality plays in the development of human nature. Our sexual nature is fundamental to being human and cannot be seen as a mere biological function. What is more, our sexual development is intimately bound up with our experiences in childhood and the origins of sexual orientation and behaviour are complex.

An Integrated View

Any modern sexual ethic that does not take account of such increases in scientific understanding about human physiology and

---

[3] Quoted in Kelsey & Kelsey, *Sacrament of Sexuality*, p. 146.

psychology will be flawed. Most atheists and agnostics will recognize this immediately, but even religious leaders accept the importance of recognizing increases in human knowledge. As Pope John Paul II puts it:

> Science can purify religion from error and superstition; religion can purify science from idolatry and false absolutes. The unprecedented opportunity we have today is for a common interactive relationship in which each discipline retains its integrity and yet is radically open to the discoveries and insights of the other.[4]

Pope Pius XII (1876–1958), one of the more conservative Popes, also emphasized the importance of taking seriously the discoveries of science:

> The observations of Hippocrates which have been recognized as exact, the discoveries of Pasteur, or Mendel's laws of heredity, do not owe the truth of their content to the moral and religious ideas of their authors ... These scientific achievements are true for the reason and to the extent that they correspond with reality.[5]

Neither of these Popes' comments were related to the sexual field, but our increased understanding of human beings as sexual creatures must be taken into account in determining sexual ethics today, just as, if one believes in God, the increased understanding of evolution must be taken into account in determining how God's interaction with the world is to be understood. Two hundred years ago, all Churches and clergy maintained that, as recorded in the Bible, God created Adam and Eve and all species of animals and plants directly.

[4] John Paul II, 1987 address marking the 300th anniversary of the publication of Newton's *Principia Mathematica*.
[5] Quoted in O. M. Liebard, ed., *Love and Sexuality: Official Catholic Teachings*, p. 168.

Darwin showed that this position was, at the least, extremely improbable and, eventually, Church teaching altered. In the same way today, increased knowledge must lead to a revision of traditional understandings of sexual ethics, although the principle of starting from an understanding of human nature is still sound.

Any adequate approach to sexuality must integrate a wide variety of insights. As Dominian puts it:

> Sexual activity has the potential first and foremost of being linked with love in a relationship with another person. In this respect it is life-giving to those involved. Secondly, it has the capacity of fertilization, which means the start of a new life. Thirdly, it is accompanied by an intense pleasure which reaches its peak in orgasm. Fourthly, though this is often forgotten, orgasm is accompanied by a relief of sexual tension. Therefore an ethic which wants to do justice to sexual activity must consider all these dimensions ... For me, sexual ethics depend on the sexual integrity of these four characteristics.[6]

A concentration on any one of these dimensions at the expense of others will result in a distorted approach. Integration of the physical, psychological, spiritual, intellectual and intimate aspects in close relationships is needed. Intimacy, trust and sharing go hand in hand, and they operate at many different levels – they can also change over time in a developing relationship. The outward expression may come in taking off our clothes and being close but this should be an expression of a sharing at a much deeper level in which we trust another human being with the gift of our inmost selves. This is a progressive process, since human beings are individuals and however much one person may love another, he or she will not fully understand all the depths of the other – it is a life-long journey of exploration.

Even those who say they are Christians may recognize that the New Testament approach to sexual morality rejected the legalistic

---

[6] Dominion & Montefiore, *God, Sex and Love*, p. 26.

approach which saw certain actions as evil in and of themselves. However, it did not abandon the idea that the moral lives of individuals matter a great deal. Specifically, all religions maintain that sexual conduct is important. The modern idea that there are no sexual boundaries and that any action is permissible provided it does not hurt anyone is totally alien to a religious vision of the purpose and destiny of human beings. As Dominian says:

> The gospel of Jesus Christ is not primarily about being good, nor about any other moralism. It is about God ... Jesus went out of his way to preach the gospel to those who were not commonly regarded as good fellows, and who were certainly not leading good lives ... He befriended them and told them the Good News, that God loved them and cared for them and forgave them. Human behaviour springs from the kind of people we are; and the gospel is about changing our nature and enabling us to be the kind of people we are meant to be ... With iron self-control, a person may be able to regulate his or her outward behaviour ... This applies to sexual behaviour as much as to other kinds of human behaviour ... [but] Self-discipline cannot change lust into love; and lust falls under condemnation in the teaching of Jesus. But not lustful people ...[7]

Sexual ethics cannot be considered apart from a wider understanding of human life and it involves a search for the truth about what it is to become fully human – this search is one that can be undertaken by atheist and religious believer. If this is accepted, then the second principle of a new approach to sexual ethics may be held to be:

> Any approach to sexual ethics must consider the whole human person and an attempt be made to seek a truthful understanding of what it is to be fully human. Aristotle and Aquinas tried to do

[7] Dominion & Montefiore, *God, Sex and Love.*

this and today the same attempt must be made, but taking account of our modern knowledge of physiology, psychology and the complexity of human relationships. If this is done, one can remain faithful to the past methodology whilst recognizing that the findings of psychology and of science must inform theological and philosophical debate.

TWELVE

Function and Freedom

The view that the primary purpose of human genitalia was for reproduction was set out in chapter 6. This led to the idea that the use of genitalia for any other purpose was 'unnatural' and represented a dysfunction: the person who used their genitalia for other purposes was doing an 'intrinsically evil' act. Some of the problems with this view were also explained – however, one of the most important weaknesses of this approach is that it is functional. It ceases to regard a human being as a unity, and instead sees the function of a part of the human body in isolation from the psychological, spiritual and physical unity that a human being represents.

Karl Marx rejected capitalism as it saw the working person in terms of his or her function as a means of generating profit. Effectively, Marx claimed that capitalism considered employees to be no more than a means to an end: they were valued solely for the function they performed. An employee was treated rather like a lathe or piece of equipment – to be used as long as it was required to produce income and to be laid aside when it could no longer serve its function.

Sadly, it must be recognized that Marx was all too frequently right in his criticism and, to the extent this applies, it is a major weakness in the capitalist system – although, of course, there is no need for it always to apply. A rejection of this approach depends on seeing every individual as autonomous and of intrinsic worth. In religious terms, each person is seen as a child of God. It can then never be right to treat a human being as a means to an end. Immanuel Kant recognized this when, in one of the formulations of his categorical imperatives, he said that human beings must always be treated as ends in themselves – they can never be 'used' for some wider end, their value is never dependent solely on the function they serve. Nowhere is this insight more important than in the sexual arena.

Once a human being fails to be seen as a person of great intrinsic worth, then it is all too easy to value him or her only for the function that is fulfilled. Someone who does this may 'have sex' with another person, valuing them, briefly, only for the sexual function they serve. Protestations of love may be made in the heat of the moment or as a way of inducing the other party to participate willingly, but these promises are usually short lived.

The reason why lust is described as a deadly sin is that it sees another person as a means to the end of our own pleasure – it fails to value the human person and simply sees the function they can perform for us. This is carried to the ultimate extreme in the case of prostitutes who are selling their services as functionaries. They are being paid to perform a service and they perform it like any other job. Most prostitutes are careful not to be emotionally involved with their clients and, indeed, set clear limits to the services they provide. For instance, it is common for prostitutes to refuse to kiss their clients on their mouth – a kiss is a gesture of intimacy which they feel is inappropriate and wholly out of place in the paid service they are rendering. A prostitute may engage in a wide range of activities and may simulate pleasure as part of the professional services she offers, but she will try to keep 'herself' uninvolved. She may perform many other sexual acts for the clients, but these acts are being done as a paid employee (albeit for the short time for which her body has been 'hired', which usually ranges from five minutes to half an hour) and the acts are devoid of personal significance. She provides a service and is not in a relationship.

Prostitutes have traditionally been regarded as outcasts from society and as fundamentally 'non-respectable'. They are seen by many as representing a threat to traditional marriage bonds but, generally, a married person will only go to a prostitute as a remedy for a problem within the marriage. It is rare for visits to a prostitute to start marriage problems – generally these visits are a symptom rather than the cause of difficulties.

Prostitutes themselves can have high ethical standards – certainly they make their bodies available for hire, but this does not mean that they do not have clear standards which they will not breach easily. A prostitute may have more integrity and be more of an individual human being before God than a priest – the prostitute is at least open and honest about what she does and there may be no other alternative open to her, whereas there can be cases where this may not apply to a priest. She may conduct her life with care and compassion for her friends and relatives and may even have a family of her own which she loves and supports. Victor Hugo's novel *Les Misérables* (on which the hit musical is based) portrays a woman forced into prostitution in order to care for her daughter – yet she remained a loving, tender, caring mother even as she died. A priest, by contrast, may be a hypocrite, pretending to be chaste and virtuous whilst, underneath, a very different picture emerges.

It is significant that the single group of people whom Jesus criticized and condemned were priests – certainly not prostitutes, whom he seemed to regard as being closer to his Father's kingdom than the respectable and pious. This was not because prostitution is morally right, but because lives of full humanity, of compassion, concern for others as well as a commitment to truth and integrity matter more than outward appearances. The person who uses a prostitute as a functionary or who has sex with a young girl purely for his own enjoyment, the man who uses a woman's body whilst failing to see her humanity, may be far more culpable than the woman whom he uses in this way.

In Leo Tolstoy's novel *Resurrection*, a young prince 'falls for' a young girl staying at the house of his aunts. He professes undying love, and she is convinced. They sleep together, which, to the girl, seems a natural and right expression of their relationship. Shortly afterwards the young man leaves to join the army and gives the girl scarcely another thought. The girl discovers she is pregnant and is thrown out by the aunts. She has no money and no way of earning a living, but she is young and attractive and is taken up by an older man as his mistress. He soon tires of her and she is forced into prostitution, gradually slipping further and further down the scale. Eventually, some years later, she is arrested and brought before magistrates – one of whom is the young prince who seduced her. He recognizes her and, for the first time, realizes the damage he has caused to her. Tolstoy's book is a moving story of his attempt to right his wrong in the face of an implacable system which prevents him doing this. This story is repeated constantly today – although rarely does the young man get to see the harvest that his action has caused. It is true that pregnancy is less likely today with the ready availability of contraception, but this does not diminish the psychological damage that can be done by treating another human being merely in terms of their function and without any depth of commitment.

To regard another human being primarily in terms of his or her function is dehumanizing. Any human being who uses another solely for their sexual gratification is degrading them in the worst possible way – they are, effectively, denying their worth as human beings. This approach must be resisted by anyone who wishes to take ethics seriously or, indeed, to value other human beings, and it will lead to a strong rejection of an instrumental view of sex, which sees sexual activity in isolation from the whole individual. Anyone who fails to do this and who fails to recognize that, in making love, there is an engagement with the whole person is effectively degrading them. It simply is not possible to treat another person as, effectively, an 'object' for one's sexual gratification without doing serious damage to the other person and to oneself.

Two persons may willingly decide to have 'recreational sex', in other words to indulge in sexual activity just for the pleasure it brings. They may humorously say:

> Sex without love is an empty experience, but as empty experiences go it is one of the best.[1]

[1] Quoted Vincent Genosi, *In Pursuit of Love*, p. 158.

This is typical of a common modern attitude but it may rest on a radical error. Both parties may consider that they are merely 'enjoying themselves', but something much deeper may be happening. In both cases they may be, effectively, denying their intrinsic worth and treating each other (and allowing themselves to be treated) merely as an object, even if they are unaware of it at the time.

One of the most troubling aspects of the survey of young people's attitudes to morality conducted in 1997 (see appendix) is that 60 per cent of those questioned considered that casual sex was morally acceptable (cf. p. 232). This response does not mean that young people act on this principle and their replies may be influenced by cultural pressure, but it fails to take into account the significance of sexual relationships.

Human beings are persons – and what is more, religious people claim that they are persons of fundamental worth before God. Someone who denies this and sees the other as of no more worth than as a sexual vehicle is denying the personhood of the other: he or she is denying their humanity. A prostitute who tries to separate her 'professional' life from her personal life may be massively hurt by the betrayal of someone who professed to genuinely love her, whilst being unmoved by 'sex acts' with her clients (even though this latter may be very difficult and most prostitutes will, inevitably, be affected by being 'used' by their clients). In fact the hurt is likely to be much deeper, as a prostitute may well feel valued and loved by her real partner and this may keep her sane, giving her a feeling of worth in a world which treats her as an object. If this sense of being valued and loved is taken away, then the destructive effect on her is very great indeed. The danger from the point of view of a prostitute or a person who 'sleeps around' regularly is that the separation between 'casual sex' (whether for money or for short-term pleasure) and genuine acts of lovemaking is difficult to achieve.

However, it is not just in the case of casual sex or prostitution that another person may be valued for their function – this can and frequently does happen in marriage as well where, for instance, the man considers he has a right to have sex with his wife. As we have seen, this idea has a long theological history and it was judged a mortal sin in the Middle Ages for a woman to refuse access. In the nineteenth century, men could divorce their wives for 'a denial of sexual congress' and if their wives were injured by a third party, the husband could sue for compensation for 'loss of consortium'. Women, by contrast, had no such reciprocal right and the nearest they came to this was when 'mental cruelty' was introduced as a ground for divorce. As recently as 1980, only three US states[2] had made the rape of a wife by her husband a crime under rape statutes – although by 1997 all US states had got round to recognizing this.

In this century, there has been a slow acceptance of women as autonomous beings with rights of their own. A man who demands to sleep with his wife or who makes her feel guilty if she does not do so is treating her as a functionary rather than as a person.

It follows from this that one should never, as a minimum, engage in sexual activity with another where this does not reflect and represent a very real commitment to the personal identity and individuality of the other. In the absence of this, we are not really engaged with another human being but rather with a human being whom we are degrading to the level of an object.

The more a person becomes promiscuous and is controlled by instinct or the desire for personal pleasure, the more he or she cease to be able to see the humanity of their partner and instead see them in terms of their function, as a means to temporarily satiating their desire. The person who sleeps with any woman (or man) who is available, the young man who is desperately anxious to 'score' and whose aim at any party he goes to is to 'pull' a different girl, or the lonely young woman who seeks love and consolation by making herself freely available are all on paths which can and often will lead to serious personal disintegration.

Everyone needs to be loved, to be cared for and to be valued – this is a feature of our common humanity. To be sure we may

[2] Nebraska, Oregon and New Jersey.

be 'tough' and 'strong'. We may make ourselves self-sufficient and convince ourselves that we do not need anyone, but in doing this we are deceiving ourselves – often as a way of coming to terms with the lack of a loving partner. However, human beings do not simply need to *receive* love, they also have a need to *give* and to *express* real love. Christianity maintains that this need to give love lies deep in the roots of our human nature. We are, literally, made to be lovers of each other.

This need to be loved and to give love is natural and right – the creation story in Genesis pictures the woman being created from the rib of *adam*, the earth creature, and there is a sense in which both man and woman are incomplete without the other. Plato, in the *Symposium*, represented this with a myth of a primordial, bisexual being, maintaining that both man and woman are incomplete without the other – the urge to love and to cherish, and to be loved and cherished, is very strong and deeply rooted. The problem is that there are few people in life who will love us unconditionally and the temptation can be, therefore, to use sex as a way of trying to bring someone to love us. Such an attempt will almost always fail. Making love can be a way of literally 'making' or 'creating' or building on an existing love. Lovemaking certainly can be an expression of a deep and committed love, but hardly ever will real love emerge merely because sexual access is given.

Sometimes people ask 'Why does no one love me?' or 'Why cannot I find a partner who will really love me?' when they fail to address the prior and more important questions of why *they* are unable to love, why *they* are unable to go out in love to others or even to love themselves. It is in loving others that we may find ourselves loved in return – but never as a 'reward' for loving, simply because those who love are those who are most love-able – most able to be loved.

The classic picture of the young man swearing undying love 'in the heat of the moment' to persuade a girl to sleep with him is followed, almost as night follows day, by his losing interest soon afterwards. This should not come as a surprise – sex here is not an expression of love or commitment, it is purely functional, and one cannot arrive at deep and committed love through functional means. Sex can be one of those immediate pleasures which many people would pay almost any price to attain but, once attained, it may be considered as worthless. History is littered with countless thousands of people who have staked career, reputation, family and everything they believe in on a few moments' pleasure, only to have everything come crashing down around their heads.

Socrates in the *Phaedrus* distinguishes between a blind, unreasonable *eros* and an *eros* which is guided by reason. The first arises when the attraction is to a beautiful body and where the desire is for momentary physical possession. Here, beauty is a means of enkindling sexual passion and satisfying it. The reasonable *eros* is similarly passionate, but it is directed more by reason and passes through three stages:[3]

1 At the lowest level, the love of beauty in one body leads one to recognize that beauty is not to be found in one thing but that beauty is found in many different guises,

2 At the second level, it is the beauty of the other person's mind which attracts. A person finds that this has an improving influence on them and may challenge and develop them.

3 At the third stage, it is the beauty of science or ideas in general that are found to be most attractive of all. This leads onto the search for pure beauty, or the perfect Form of beauty which, in Christian terms, is expressed most deeply in God.[4]

The second stage analysed by Socrates is important – true love will only develop when what is loved in the other is not the bodily 'packaging'. This may, it is true, be the initial attraction, but if this is

[3] Outlined in the *Symposium*.
[4] The Franciscan tradition, in particular, expresses this. See the work of St Bonaventure. In particular, refer to Paul Rout, *Francis and Bonaventure*, Fount Christian Thinkers, Fount Paperbacks, 1996.

all there is it will quickly fade. Genuine, deep love will only develop where the love is of the deeper self, the real person behind the exterior, and it will take time, care and trouble to discover this deeper person. This is one reason that hasty marriages are less likely to succeed, because the parties do not have the time necessary to get to know each other at the deeper level which is an essential precondition for real love emerging. Most of us find it difficult to know ourselves, and to get to know another human being will usually take a long time. There is an old Victorian saying: 'Marry in haste, repent at leisure.' Like many old sayings it contains much wisdom – to commit oneself to another person for the whole of one's life in the knowledge that the attractive bodily packaging will age and wither, that the fine young man will develop a paunch and be picking his toe nails on the bed in 20 years' time or will be sprawled in front of the television drinking beer, that in 40 years he may be incontinent and bedridden should be enough to give any young couple pause for thought. It is only if what is valued is the deeper humanity of the individual that real love can occur and only then is there any possibility of this love enduring through all the 'changes and chances of this fleeting world'.

Real lovemaking will seek not the pleasure of the self but the joy and development of the other. It is an expression of passion, love and commitment which should not have a selfish aim but which should be directed towards thinking of the other person. Paradoxically, it will be in giving joy and pleasure that joy and pleasure will be found – but as a by-product, never as an end in itself. Real love can be costly as it may mean not holding on to someone but freeing them to move to a new stage in life. This is why possessiveness or jealousy are such destructive emotions, as they come from a selfish wish to be made happy oneself rather than to ensure the happiness of the beloved.

The third principle for a new approach to sexual ethics can now be established, namely:

Sexual relationships should always recognize the role of the other person involved as a free, autonomous human being and no human being may use another as a means to the end of his or her sexual gratification. Sex should always be a free act, a gift of intimacy, commitment and trust by one person to another. It should never be coerced, whether mentally or physically and should always express the depth of the relationship rather than being a means to try to develop a relationship. The pleasure involved should come as a by-product of the gift of love and tenderness, never as an end in itself.

THIRTEEN

Mystery and Taboo

In Victorian times, there was a considerable measure of prudery about sex. Sex was never discussed in polite society and young women often had almost no idea what was going to 'happen to them' on their wedding night, except for dire hints that may have been given by their mothers – which often were of the 'Lie back and think of England' variety. Piano legs were often covered up because they were too suggestive and, at a dinner party, guests would ask for 'white meat' rather than breast of chicken. Today this prudery is alien – countless films, videos, popular songs, TV shows and teenage and adult magazines deal with sex in great detail. Articles are written on how to achieve multiple orgasms and 'performance', both for the man and the woman, becomes an objective which is often discussed more or less openly. Teenage magazines make sexual facts available to young people in a way that has never happened before in history, and older men attend sex clinics to boost their flagging powers. Many people are willing to talk freely, at least to close friends, about the technical side of sexual matters and about the difficulties that arise.

In the last twenty years there has been a considerable improvement in sex education in schools. Most young people today have been provided with books, have been shown films and have been given the chance to discuss all aspects of the biology of sex. They are, by about 13 or 14, familiar with the human reproductive system, periods, erections, 'wet dreams', contraception and the like. The detailed knowledge provided to them is at a level to which their parents would never have been exposed. Also, there is a frankness and openness which avoids at least some of the embarrassment of talking about sex and the great deal of information means that teenage pregnancies are rare in spite of the high rate of sexual activity by many young people.

However, this increased information is often given out of context – it is entirely factual and value-free and, at best (or rather at worst), it strips away from sexuality any idea of mystery. The ecstatic meeting of two people in acts of tender, caring, committed 'love-making' is reduced to a physical process little different from the animals in the farmyard. One can 'let light in on magic' and, by so doing, destroy everything that is precious and worthwhile, destroy the real meaning of what is taking place.

I am reminded of the story of an old, clever but mentally ill man who used to pick flowers and then pluck off every part, naming them as he went. He could identify the anther, stamen, petal, sepal, etc., with great precision – but he had no feeling for the unity of the flower, no comprehension of its beauty or its deeper meaning in the overall scheme of things. He analysed away all that was important and became obsessed with trivia. All too often, the same happens in the sexual field.

Human activities can be analysed away until their real meaning disappears. Human brains can be analysed in terms of their neural activity and the fact that persons are 'more' than their physical make-up can be easily ignored. Religious mysteries, also, can be destroyed by undue analysis. It is all too easy to analyse religious words and profound experiences like those found in worship, ritual or prayer and, in so doing, lose sight of the true meaning.

Wittgenstein recognized this in his rejection of James Frazer's *The Golden Bough* (1890). Frazer was an anthropologist who analysed the myths and religious practices of 'primitive societies' without ever visiting these societies or spending time with them. Frazer's perspective was that of a late-Victorian, Anglican Englishman who could conceive that no other framework but his own, rational, scientific world view could make sense. Applying this to supposedly primitive rituals such as the rain dance or the feast of the Beltane fires, Frazer misunderstood them and attempted to show how primitive they were – maintaining that they were a stage in human development before the higher, scientific understanding could be accepted. Wittgenstein rejected this utterly. He maintained that Frazer had not begun to understand the 'depth grammar' of these festivals and rituals, which were far more profound and complicated than Frazer allowed. Wittgenstein's view of philosophy was that it had no business laying down what could and could not be said – instead it should 'leave everything as it is' and should content itself with providing a perspicuous (truthful/insightful) understanding of complexities. Many of the most profound mysteries and experiences of human life could not be explained and, if explanation was attempted, they would be trivialized.

Wittgenstein's sensitivity, in contrast to Frazer's superficiality, can point to a helpful way of looking at sex today. Sex is, or should be, a mystery in which two people who love each other and who recognize each other's full humanity can express and deepen their love. There is, indeed, something 'religious' and 'holy' about the union of two people. However, the mystery, the sacredness of the sexual bond can easily be trivialized and destroyed by crude emphasis on function. In fact, this is what most modern language about sex sets out to do – it tears away the mystery, it seeks to look inside the holy of holies and, when it finds nothing therein, concludes that there is nothing there. This, however, is an impoverished understanding of reality or of the role of mystery in our lives.

There are many places in life which fill us, unless we are desperately cynical, with awe and wonder, places when we are forced to be silent and to be still. Birth is one of these places, and so too is death – although death is today too easily 'sanitized' and the mystery and awe removed. Religion is one of the last bastions where awe and wonder is preserved – but it is too easy for philosophers and theologians to explain away the mysterious, to analyse and to question and then to wonder why they are seeking the Snark which has the curious feature of disappearing whenever one tries to capture it.[1] Rudolf Otto talked of the awe and wonder as one approaches 'the holy' and of the '*mysterium tremendum et fascinans*' which the idea of God represents. The rituals of some Churches, notably the Eastern Orthodox or the plainchant of Benedictine monks, preserve this sense of 'otherness', of something alien to our contemporary, scientific way of thinking. The same applies to the mystery of sex.

Newspaper headlines will often use terminology which reduces sex to a merely physical, not to say animal, level. They will talk, for instance, of 'bonking' or 'f★★★ing' or of how many lovers a person will have. Indeed, many newspapers prosper by catering for the titillation factor to which sexual stories give rise. Writing about sexual activity in an explicit, factual way is one of the most effective means of denying the humanity and vulnerability of the participants. It is to rip aside the veils of mystery and to leave everything exposed – except all that is really important disappears as soon as the element of mystery is removed.

Taboos have traditionally surrounded many areas of sex, and taboos are important means of safeguarding mystery. They are a way of marking 'holy ground' of indicating that one should 'take off one's shoes' when approaching something sacred. To tread over taboos with the hobnailed boots of analysis and language is to destroy them. Mystery is easily destroyed and it is preserved only with difficulty and, once the taboos have been removed, it is likely that the mystery and all it conveys will disappear as well. The Bible recognizes this, saying quite explicitly that a son shall not uncover the nakedness of his mother and, if he does so, he is to be put to death – there is something sacred here which should not be lightly trampled on. Again, the Bible talks of Adam 'knowing' (*yada*) Eve[2] – indeed this word 'to know' one's wife is frequently used instead of the cruder 'having sex with'. However, the difference between the words is important – it is not simply that the former is more

---

[1] Cf. Lewis Carroll's *The Hunting of the Snark*.
[2] Genesis 4:1.

sensitive than the latter. To talk of a man 'having sex with' his wife may debase both partners and completely miss what is really happening in this intimate interchange. When a man 'knows' his wife there is much more being recognized in the interchange that is taking place.

Søren Kierkegaard (1813–1855) distinguished between objective and subjective truth. Objective truths can be communicated directly – these are the sort of factual truths that can be learned from books or in a classroom. Young people today are given a great deal of factual, objective information relating to the sexual arena, but this takes no account of subjective knowledge. Subjective knowledge has to do with what sexual activity means for me, as an individual. What it means to share myself at an intimate and vulnerable level with another human being; what it means to love another person and to value their individual and unique humanity. Such knowledge is not easily communicated – which is why the importance of example is so great. The example of a loving, committed and sexually relaxed mother and father will be the best way of communicating this subjective knowledge. By contrast, a child who has been sexually abused by a parent or who sees parents who are manipulative or who 'use' each other will find it very difficult to reach an understanding of the true meaning of human sexuality.

Sex education in schools, although in some ways admirable, does not recognize the difference between mere sexual knowledge or what the biblical term *yada* means. Helmut Thielicke puts it this way:

'How shall I tell it to my child?' This question is usually uttered with a sigh, which indicates that giving this information is painful and embarrassing to the parents. At the same time the same embarrassment and reserve in the attitude of young people toward their parents manifests itself as soon as questions of sex are raised – even in situations where there is otherwise a good relationship of trust between them and their parents ... the child or teenager is given a pamphlet, or the instruction is left to the school ... What attitude towards sexual knowledge betrays itself in this tendency to give sexual enlightenment from a safe distance? ... The inhibition is caused by something the parents remember: they know from their own past that a young person is not yet capable of understanding the sex act as the 'expression' of ultimate human communication, and that therefore at his first acquaintance with it he will think of it as something indecent, something of which he would never imagine his parents capable ... This crisis of mutual confidence as well as the shame of being connected with an act which their children would not think them capable of, causes the parents to shy away from taking the initiative in giving instruction.

Consequently, the sexual act, which is the very thing the youngster wants to get in the clear about, can be conceived of only as something animal which – for some puzzling reason – the parents engage in despite the fact that they are loved and respected human beings.[3]

T. S. Eliot says that one can 'have the experience and miss the meaning'. More factual information about sex does not contribute to any greater degree of understanding of the meaning involved – 'information' and 'understanding' inhabit different dimensions. The child encounters sex not as a mystery which hides something good, but as something that is forbidden, dark and 'secret', or, to the extent it comes into the open by means of information, as something broadly animal, exciting and to be desired on its own account. Theilicke says – and it is a profound point – that:

> The practice of giving sexual instruction, or the omission of it, is a mirror of the marriage itself and very often a judgement on it.[4]

It is not possible to undergo 'instruction' on the real meaning of sex, just as it is not possible to learn what real love is except by

---

[3] Thielicke, *The Ethics of Sex*, pp. 70–1.
[4] Thielicke, p. 73.

experience. Great literature, poetry or art may be better mediums of expression than appeal to biology. It is for this reason that appeal to 'rules' in the sexual arena is so very unhelpful – the rules frequently seem irrelevant and an imposition by the older generation on the young of norms which the older generation themselves often do not accept.

Brendan Callaghan, SJ, emphasizes the sense of mystery when he writes:

> Sex, it seems to me, remains forever mysterious – and that's good news. Over the last couple of generations we have come to know a lot more about the physiology, psychology, sociology and the history of sex. We have identified some of the patterns of embryonic sexual development, and seem to be on the brink of identifying the roles of genetics and experience in mediating sexual variability ... But all that *is* clear is that, at the end of the day, our sexuality is mysterious – in the sense that we never fully understand our sexual selves ... we are always open to being puzzled, surprised, elated, downcast, to having our relationships, our patterns of life and our commitments unexpectedly strengthened, or just as unexpectedly thrown into confusion. We may know more about how our sexual mechanisms operate, but we are all still beginners at learning about the relational power of sex – or perhaps that should be the sexual power of relationships.[5]

Sacrilege involves the desecration of the holy, it means profaning that which is 'other' and bringing it down to the level of the mundane world. Sacrilege consists in playing with the mystery in order to exploit it.[6] The same happens in the case of sex – those who destroy the mystery of the sexual act, the mystery of the inter-communion of two human beings who 'make' or 'create' love, profane it and destroy that which is really important. This

---

[5] *The Guardian*, November 1996.
[6] Cf. Thielicke, p. 78.

destruction can be achieved by concentration on 'performance' rather than relationship, and also by concentration on detached moral rules which fail to see the deeper humanity of the individuals involved. This is one of those things which are understood by the simple but not by the clever – the so-called clever man thinks, when he has picked the flower apart, he has understood the flower. In fact he has destroyed it.

The Four Principles of the New Approach

The final principle can now be added to complete the four principles for a new approach to sexual ethics:

1 Psychology has made clear the intimate link between sexuality, personality and human development as well as the need for human integration. Sexuality is an essential part of human nature and each person has to come to wholeness by being able to accept and balance the different aspects of their nature. Sexuality and spirituality may be seen to be connected. The ability to love and to accept love, to form relationships and to enter into mature, adult sexual bonds depend to a larger extent on the experiences one has as a young child. Early experiences can distort the development process and can cause adults to be psychologically immature. The impact of parents and a warm, stable, loving home environment is important to psychological well-being. If this is absent, distortions are likely to result which may not be resolvable without help later in life. The negative view of human sexual nature deriving from the Christian tradition needs to be rejected and a positive approach taken to the wholeness of human experience in giving and receiving love.

2 Any approach to sexual ethics must consider the whole human person and an attempt be made to seek a truthful understanding of what it is to be fully human. Aristotle and Aquinas tried to do this and today the same attempt must be made, but taking account of our modern knowledge of physiology, psychology and the

complexity of human relationships. If this is done, one can remain faithful to the past methodology whilst recognizing that the findings of psychology and of science must inform theological and philosophical debate.

3   Sexual relationships should always recognize the role of the other person involved as a free, autonomous human being and no human being may use another as a means to the end of his or her sexual gratification. Sex should always be a free act, a gift of intimacy, commitment and trust by one person to another. It should never be coerced, whether mentally or physically and should always express the depth of the relationship rather than being a means to try to develop a relationship. The pleasure involved should come as a by-product of the gift of love and tenderness, never as an end in itself.

4   Lovemaking between two people is something 'deep' and mysterious – it, like birth and death, is one of the great mysteries of life and concentration on the mechanics of the act without an appreciation of its role in the wider relationship misses its true significance. No philosophic analysis will be adequate to capture the full mystery of love nor will any set of rules meet all the complexities of human relationships.

Questions for Discussion

1   Do you consider there is anything wrong with a man saying he loves someone in order to get them to sleep with him when this is not true? Give your reasons.

2   Karl Marx thought that capitalists exploited workers. Is there anything wrong with exploiting someone else? If so, how might one person exploit another in a sexual relationship either (a) within marriage, or (b) outside marriage?

3   Do you consider that there is any essential difference between having sex with someone and cooking them a good dinner? Why?

4   Do you believe that all human beings share a common human nature? Give reasons for your answers. Why is this question important?

5   How do you think education about sex for 12–14 year olds should be conducted? What are the main things that a teacher or parents should try to get them to understand?

6   What is the difference between objective and subjective truth? Give examples.

7   Read the Song of Songs and then explain what you think it is about.

8   What does it mean to love someone? Has love got anything to do with sex and if so what is the connection?

9   How do Freud and Jung's views on the importance of sex differ?

10 List five ways in which an adult's sexual life may be influenced by experiences in early childhood.

11 What do you think are the strengths and weaknesses of a religious person deciding to be celibate?

12 Paedophilia is morally wrong and desperately harmful – however, how might such behaviour be explained (even though not excused)?

13 Are prostitutes morally wicked? Give reasons for your answer.

14 Do you agree or disagree with the four principles suggested that should underpin any modern understanding of sexual ethics? Give your reasons for or against and suggest alternatives if appropriate.

PART 3

DEALING WITH CURRENT PROBLEMS

FOURTEEN

Cybersex, Masturbation and Fantasy

Cybersex

Many of the new developments in electronic technology over the last twenty years have been promoted and developed by those providing erotic material. In the late 1970s when few American homes had videos, 75 per cent of all videos sold were in this category. *Adult Video News*, a Californian trade publication, estimates that rentals of adult video tapes through video stores in 1995 were worth $3.1 billion, with mail-order sales worth another $1 billion. In Germany, 40 per cent of all videos rented are erotic. According to *The Economist*, in American hotels, at least half the annual $175m revenue from pay-per-view films comes from adult or erotic movies.[1] With the increase in the availability of cable television and satellite TV, both of which offer many channels, the popularity of 'adult' channels seems likely to increase still further.

It may, however, be that the Internet is likely to be the most successful provider of erotic material. The Internet has given everyone with a telephone line the ability to access images, text and voice messages from anywhere in the world and, increasingly, to interact with the sender. Many so-called 'adult' services are now available on the Internet, providing sexually explicit images and text at relatively low cost. For those who access these messages, they represent a considerable improvement over photographs, videos or magazines because:

---

[1] *The Economist*, 4 January, 1997.

- They can be continually changed.
- A much wider range of material is available and by accessing specific sites specific tastes can be catered for.
- They are much more life-like – 12 images a second can be down loaded compared with 30 for television pictures, and although this means the pictures are a little jerky, nevertheless the quality is adequate.
- They can be interactive as, through the use of video-conferencing facilities, a 'client' can talk to the girl at the other end of the telephone line – who may, of course, be on the other side of the world.

Five million people a day access the Playboy Internet site and Tony Lynn, president of Playboy Entertainment, considers the company's Internet site as 'potentially our most important revenue earner'. The profits in providing sexually explicit materials via the Internet are considerable. Customers pay in one of two ways – either by the cost of the call or by credit card. In order to avoid regulatory restrictions on the provision of 'exotic' material, many companies now operate from far away places where there are almost no rules – these can be accessed down any telephone line. The International Telephone Communication union (ITU) estimates that 1.5 per cent of all international telephone calls are sex calls. These calls can, the ITU claims, aid development. *The Economist* quotes the example of Guyana in Latin America which has an annual GDP of \$2000 per head. In the last five years it has increased its volume of international calls from 23.8 million minutes to 139.7 million minutes – an annual growth rate of 56 per cent. As a result, its income from telecommunications is now \$130 million or 40 per cent of the country's GDP – this is equivalent to \$700 per household. For a poor country this is a hugely significant sum.

Customers who dial the video-conferencing facilities operated by Virtual Dreams in the US pay \$5.99 per minute. The average call lasts for 13 minutes thus giving rise to a bill for \$78. The girl who answers the call receives \$25 per hour – she can be seen by the client, but the girl cannot see the client. Virtual Dreams generates $700,000 per month from this service. Forrester Research, a Boston consultancy company, estimates that 10 per cent of all revenue on the Internet comes from cybersex.

The reasons for using cybersex facilities may vary – some clients may use the service just for the titillation factor, others may be lonely and unable, for psychological reasons with their roots in childhood, to form adult sexual bonds of their own. However, the demand is undoubtedly considerable and a number of issues arise which are not often addressed in moral textbooks. One of the more obvious issues is whether regulations to discourage the use of cybersex facilities should be introduced. Britain and Germany have both recently applied restrictions and in some cases, particularly in the case of erotic photographs of young children which may be against the law, police make efforts to trace those sending and those receiving the images.

In 1990 in Britain 70–80 per cent of all premium-rate telephone calls were to 'adult services', but this percentage has now decreased, due to tighter regulation, to a very small figure. However, it is easier to regulate telephone calls than the Internet – the continual technical advances and the reluctance of most governments to censor material makes regulation difficult. What is more, the system itself is designed to use multiple alternative pathways and this makes control much more difficult. When demand is so high for sexually explicit material and the potential profits are so considerable, it is always likely that new technological developments will circumvent any regulations. As Mr Guess, the Chief Executive of Virtual Dreams says:

> The two contents that drive technology are warfare and sex ...
> and sex generates the revenues.[2]

Those accessing cybersex facilities may do so for various reasons, but two of the possible reasons will be looked at below.

---

[2] Quoted in *The Economist*, 4 January, 1997.

Masturbation

Masturbation is common amongst adolescents, but is also a feature of the lives of many older men and women – even though they may rarely discuss this with anyone and may feel guilty about it. There is no specific biblical injunction against masturbation except a text in Genesis 38 which is dealt with below. Masturbation has traditionally been condemned by Christian moralists on the following grounds:

a) It is held to be against biblical teaching particularly as there is a waste of 'seed'. In the days when the male seed was considered as the individual and the womb was merely the 'nest' in which it developed, it is obvious that the waste of seed could be looked at as a serious manner.
b) It is held to be neither procreative nor unitive and since these are held by some to be the main purposes of the sexual act, neither are fulfilled.

Doctors also used to consider masturbation to be harmful. Freud considered masturbation one of the most common expressions of neurosis and it has been associated with blindness, consumption, low intelligence, impotence and digestive disorders. The emphasis in discussions of masturbation tends to focus on male masturbation, which is particularly common among adolescent young men, although it extends well into later age. The Kinsey studies indicate that 90 per cent or more of males engage in such practices at least at some times and it may be that the figure is higher than this as some people are reluctant to admit it. Female masturbation is less common (approximately 50 per cent of women engage in this activity) and it does not feature in the traditional Christian literature – perhaps because men wrote the rules and men never imagined women getting pleasure from the sexual act.

Whatever the rights and wrongs of the issue, two points must be recognized:

- As a matter of fact, most individuals do masturbate at some point in their lives.
- Those Christians who do take Church teaching seriously are often inflicted with considerable feelings of guilt, shame and negativity after masturbation. Traditionally this was built upon and increased by priests in the confessional who solemnly told people what a grave sin they were committing with little or no recognition of the psychological complexities involved.

The three grounds for rejecting masturbation set out above will be examined in turn.

a) The Bible

As has already been said, there is no biblical prohibition against masturbation. The only reference to it is as follows:

> Onan ... spilled his semen on the ground. And what he did was displeasing in the sight of the Lord, and he slew him. (Genesis 38:9–10)

This gave rise to masturbation being described as 'onanism', yet this is a good example of how a biblical quotation can be taken out of context. To understand the full passage it is first necessary to recognize the background. This is clearly expressed in the following text which, although it is dated from a later time, nevertheless explains clearly the practice which gave rise to God's anger:

> If brothers dwell together, and one of them dies and has no son, the wife of the dead shall not be married outside the family to a stranger; her husband's brother shall go into her, and take her as his wife, and perform the duty of a husband's brother to her. And the first son she bears shall succeed to the name of the brother who is dead, that his name may not be blotted out ... (Deuteronomy 25:5–6)

The situation is clear – the surviving brother must sleep with his dead brother's wife and produce children. The first son born as a result of this act then inherits from the dead brother. This is a clear obligation on the surviving brother, and if he refused and says 'I do not wish to take her', then:

> ... his brother's wife shall go up to him in the presence of the elders, and pull his sandal off his foot, and spit in his face and she shall answer and say 'So shall it be done to the man who does not build up his brother's house.' (Deuteronomy 25:9)

Given this background, the full text of the Onan text above becomes understandable:

> And Judah took a wife for Er his first born, and her name was Tamar. But Er, Judah's first born, was wicked in the sight of the Lord, and the Lord slew him. Then Judah said to Onan, 'Go to your brother's wife, and perform the duty of a brother-in-law to her, and raise up offspring for your brother.' But Onan knew that the offspring would not be his; so when he went into his brother's wife he spilled the semen on the ground, lest he should give offspring to his brother. And what he did was displeasing in the sight of the Lord ... (Genesis 38:6–10)

This passage, therefore, has nothing to do with masturbation – it was due to the failure to fulfil the duty due to the brother's widow.

b) Natural Law

The traditional understanding of Natural Law prohibits masturbation because it is a misuse of genitalia whose *telos* or purpose should be directed, at least partly, to the creation of children. The Aristotelian background to this approach has already been examined. Once it is accepted that genitalia have a function of their own (namely procreation) then their use for any purpose that does not at least include the possibility of procreation is to sin and to misuse the organs. This is, therefore, held to be a sin against God as God did not intend genitalia to be used in this way.

As we have seen, the weakness of this understanding is clear – human organs cannot be separated out and held to have functions of their own. Human beings are complex, and bodies, psyche and emotions are closely integrated. Making love to someone is not simply a matter of using a particular organ – it is a question of sharing one's body at a deep level and it involves love and trust. It also – and this the Christian Church has never recognized except very recently other than to disapprove of it – is intensely pleasurable. If God made human beings and made human bodies such that making love is one of the most pleasurable activities that a human being can undertake, then to hold that this pleasure is wrong or sinful seems a distorted view of God's gift. Obviously, sexual pleasure is best expressed between two people but where, for whatever reason, this is not possible or not appropriate, it is hard to see why masturbation should be regarded as, in itself, sinful.

c) Separation of the unitive and procreative acts, contraception and IVF

Anglican, Methodist, Baptist and other Protestant Churches see making love as uniting the two parties and accept that a couple may wish to plan their families and may use artificial contraception to do so. There is no reason, therefore, why a couple should not come together to make love without wishing for a child to result. Similarly, atheists and agnostics will generally see no moral problem in the use of birth control devices. This position is, however, rejected by the Roman Catholic magisterium and understanding their view can also aid in understanding their condemnation of masturbation. The papal encyclical *Humanae Vitae* said that there is:

> ... an inseparable connection, willed by God and unable to be broken by man on his own initiative, between the two meanings of the conjugal act: the unitive meaning and the procreative meaning.

155

The document says that masturbation is 'another sign of the dissociation' of the two meanings of the sexual act since it is neither unitive nor procreative. Traditionally masturbation has been regarded as a grave sin. The Catholic Church taught:

> ... all cases of masturbation are objectively grave moral evils; every act of masturbation done with sufficient reflection and full consent is mortally sinful.[3]

Central to the current Roman Catholic position is that making love involves both the uniting of husband and wife and the possibility of procreation. Many recent statements have emphasized that under no circumstances may these two be separated. It is for this reason that the Catholic Church condemns artificial birth control as, whilst making love using birth control may still unite husband and wife, the possibility of procreation is eliminated. This is also one of the reasons for the condemnation of masturbation as procreation cannot take place – even when the semen obtained by the male masturbating is being used to fertilize his wife's egg as part of IVF. IVF (In Vitro Fertilization) involves taking eggs out of a woman, fertilizing these on a slide using the partner's sperm and re-implanting some of them in the woman, and is rejected by the Catholic Church partly, but only partly, because of this view. As the document *Donum Vitae* puts it:

> Fertilization achieved outside the bodies of the couple remains by this very fact deprived of the meaning and values which are expressed in the language of the body and in the union of human persons.[4]

---

[3] Cf. Phillipe Keane, *Sexual Morality: A Catholic Perspective*, 1980, p. 59. The idea of 'sufficient reflection and full consent' is vitally important to the Catholic view of sin – mortal sins (which traditionally have been seen as condemning people to Hell) were only those sins knowingly and quite deliberately undertaken in the full knowledge that they were evil. This has led some theologians to claim that very few mortal sins are committed as very few people act with 'sufficient reflection and full consent'.

[4] *Donum Vitae*, Section ll B4b.

The document warns against any use by doctors of medical technology to bring about pregnancy other than by 'normal' lovemaking:

> ... it sometimes happens that a medical procedure technologically replaces the conjugal act in order to obtain procreation which is neither its result nor its fruit. In this case the medical act is not, as it should be, at the service of conjugal union but rather appropriates to itself the procreative function and thus contradicts the dignity and inalienable rights of the spouses and of the child to be born.[5]

In other words, it is being held that because the wife's egg is not impregnated as part of natural lovemaking, this undermines the 'meaning and value' and the 'dignity' which is essential in the creation of a child. However, this position can readily be challenged:

1 A couple who cannot have children without artificial help, such as that involved in IVF, may well be drawn closer by the difficulties and trauma that can be involved in the prolonged tests and procedures needed for IVF techniques to work. In the case of some couples who have used this technique the wife has helped the husband masturbate to produce the semen that will be used to fertilize her egg. There is no basis, therefore, for the blanket assertion that such procedures necessarily undermine the 'meaning and value' of normal lovemaking.

2 As our knowledge of the human genome increases, there is increasingly strong evidence that many diseases have genetic origins and many of us carry the genes which will make death from specific diseases highly probable. As an example, 1 in 25 people from a Caucasian background carries the gene which makes cystic fibrosis (CF) likely. A woman who knows she is a carrier and wants to have

[5] *Donum Vitae*, Section ll B7.

children must conceive with a non-CF male to avoid her child carrying the defect. Genetic alteration is also possible as a way of overcoming the problem. Down's syndrome, Huntington's disease; Alzheimer's, colon cancer, some forms of breast cancer and muscular dystrophy also have genetic origins. These diseases do not occur by chance but often because of genetic defects – and science gives us the ability to substantially reduce their incidence. However, this may well involve increased use of IVF if sperm or egg is altered prior to fertilization, and to rule this out partly because the sperm has to be obtained through masturbation is counter-intuitive.

The claim that the 'unitive and procreative' sides of making love cannot be separated rests on an unargued assertion. This is assumed to be God's will, but no evidence is given for this nor is there any argument advanced to support this. As medical science advances and as the pressure of human population growth continues, it may well be that God, if one believes in God, has entrusted human beings with the need to maintain a sensible population balance so as to care for the whole of God's world. God has created a world of profound beauty and complexity and has given human beings minds to enquire into its workings and in many ways to manipulate the environment in which we live. To claim, without argument, that in the unique case of human sexuality the two stated purposes of making love cannot be separated is a good example of bringing an assumption about the conclusion of the argument into the premise.

d) Working from the Facts
The first of the three principles set out in the previous section emphasized the need to study the facts of human nature in order to seek a true understanding of what being human involves. We now recognize, in a way that previous theologians would never have considered, that human bodies are complex. Sexually, the human body responds to a wide variety of different stimuli – not all of which are physical. As a detailed example, male orgasms are known

to result relatively easily and sperm is discharged as a result – indeed there is a direct link between the release of sperm and the pleasure that comes from a male orgasm. However, females are different: it is perfectly possible, and indeed with some women common, for them to rarely if ever experience orgasm. This may be because their partners are inconsiderate; it may be because, biologically, orgasms do not come easily or it may be that the whole setting of bodily union is closer to mere sex than lovemaking. Women integrate the whole experience of being close to someone they love with the sexual act itself, and if they feel 'used' by the man or they feel that love is absent, then an orgasm may well not result.

A man has traditionally been held to have rights over his wife's body. Many men have taken full advantage of this right – sometimes using their wives as sexual objects with no thought to the love that should be involved or to the woman's physical needs. Yet such acts are, according to traditional Church teaching, morally acceptable because they are made within marriage and are open to procreation. The complexities of our shared humanity, our physical needs as sexual beings and our bodies all need to be recognized in a way which few if any theologians have seriously attempted. Making love can be intensely pleasurable and can bring together those who love each other as well as developing their relationship, but mere 'sex' can be devoid of meaning and significance and both can occur within and outside marriage.

It is one thing for St Augustine or St Thomas Aquinas to have neglected to take these issues into account – in their culture and time it is hardly surprising. Today, however, any 17-year-old knows more about human bodies than either of these two great theologians or, indeed, than many celibate priests (although almost every celibate priest and nun will themselves have had to wrestle with the problems of their own sexuality and with the issue of masturbation – even if they are reluctant to admit it). If sexual ethics is to continue to be engaged in a search for truth rather than just accepting what previous generations have handed down, then it must take into account not just modern understandings of science but also knowledge of human bodies, psychology and the emotional and affective side of human beings.

One will look in vain in Church documents for consideration of the meaning, biology or purpose of orgasms. Women can have an orgasm either internally or externally through pressure on her clitoris. (As far as is known, the clitoris is the only bodily organ whose sole purpose is pleasure.) There is also a link between the sensitivity of a woman's breasts and her stimulation prior to orgasm. If one is to argue from an empirical understanding of human nature and to look at the purpose of sexuality (as Aristotle, Aquinas and the Roman Catholic tradition have always maintained), then these factors need to be taken into account in a broader understanding of sexuality. Those who react against discussion of such issues need to examine their own presuppositions, which may well stem from a Platonic view which denigrates the importance of the body and the physical aspect of our common humanity.

A survey in the UK among young people indicates that only 6.4 per cent of females and 10.2 per cent of males consider masturbation to be a morally wrong act. Most acts of masturbation are, according to research in the United States, conducted by teenage boys (the figure of 90 per cent has already been referred to). Today, males mature as early or earlier than ever in the past, yet marriage is much later. In the Middle Ages, marriage was common at 14 for boys and at 13 for girls. By 14, most girls would be pregnant and the life expectancy would be, perhaps, 40 years. It is not surprising today, therefore, that masturbation is common and, perhaps, normal in the absence of any other sexual outlet. We now know that various species of apes and a variety of other animals also masturbate and whilst it may be a mark of loneliness and may, if continued into adulthood as the sole method of sexual expression, be a reflection of a distortion of the personality, it is difficult to see the grounds for universal condemnation.

It may be that masturbation is morally neutral – a natural act which aids self development at a crucial stage in life. Katchadourian puts it this way:

Masturbation plays an important part in ... development ... As a vehicle for learning about the sexual aspects of one's body and one's self, masturbation continues to play a useful role throughout adulthood.[6]

The Catholic psychiatrist Jack Dominian shares this view, and sees no moral problem with masturbation in adolescence and even in adults maintains that the situation must be taken into account.[7] He recognizes that solitary masturbation may have a positive role in relieving tension, and mutual masturbation by husband and wife or by two partners of the same sex may be appropriate if love is present.

The only problem may arise if, on a longer term basis, masturbation becomes a substitute for sexual relations between a loving couple and, therefore, may become a denial of the essential meaning of sexuality, which has to do with developing a deep relationship. To close oneself off from the possibility of such a relationship may well lead to masturbation and this may then be a sign of a wider problem.

Fantasy

Almost every human being, at some stages in their lives, engages in sexual fantasies. These fantasies may be of different types – they may be fantasies about a partner who a person is missing because they are apart. They may be fantasies which the person involved may never intend to act out but which express hidden desires – for instance about members of the same sex or about a sexual partner dressing in a certain way. They may be fantasies as a result of watching certain films or videos. They may be fantasies that dominate the thinking of the person concerned and can lead onto their being acted out. In short, there may be many different sources.

To deny the fantasy or dream world of human beings is to deny an important part of our shared humanity, and it may well be that

[6] Quoted in Kelsey & Kelsey, *Sacrament of Sexuality*.
[7] Dominian & Montefiore, *God, Sex and Love*, p. 28.

dreams and fantasy are ways developed by the human brain of coming to terms with psychological or other difficulties. We now know the complexity of the forces involved in developing into mature adults able to give and receive love to others, and psychology has made clear how easy it is for the development process to be disrupted.

One of the respondents to the questionnaire set out at the end of this book, in reply to the question as to whether masturbation was morally wrong, replied: 'It depends who one is thinking about when one does it.' This comment shows insight, as sometimes we can learn something about ourselves which we may recognize as a problem which needs to be overcome. Fantasies, for instance, that involve violence or young children may well point to a problem in our sexual development which may need to be dealt with. Such fantasies are morally wrong as well as indicating a psychological problem because they clearly point towards abuse.

If fantasies become a substitute for enduring sexual bonds with others, then they may sometimes be a guide to distortions that have been brought about by events early in life and which one may need to work through with a trained counsellor. A married person who persistently engages in sexual fantasy may come to see this as a problem in their married life which should preferably be resolved. To try to suppress the fantasy rather than to come to terms with the background issues which give rise to the fantasy may be to miss the point.

The more an individual lives in a fantasy world, the less they may really relate to others and this may be an indication of relational problems that need to be overcome. This may be a growing danger with the use of 'virtual reality' machines which, as they are developed, may enable a person to engage in graphic and seemingly realistic fantasy of having sex with a wide variety of partners. However, these experiences are synthetic and they divorce the sexual act from the bonds of intimacy and love to which they properly belong and they may well be dehumanizing.

FIFTEEN

Friendship and
Sex Before Marriage

Friendship

The importance of close bonds between human individuals is recognized by some of the greatest Christian saints. For instance, St Augustine, writing about a friend who had died 25 years previously, said:

> Well has someone said of his friend that he is half of his soul. For I thought that my soul and his soul were but one soul in two bodies. Therefore my life was a horror to me, because I would not live as a half.[1]

St Gregory of Nyssa, one of the greatest of the early Church fathers, wrote of his friendship with Basil in these terms:

> It seems as though there was but one soul between us, having two bodies. And if we must not believe those who say that all things are in all things, yet you must believe this, that we were both in each one of us, and the one in the other ...[2]

Both these saints clearly had very close, not to say intimate, friends and such friendships were not confined to same sex friendships.

[1] *The Confessions of St Augustine*, trans. John Ryan, Image Books, 1960, book 4 chapter 6.
[2] Quoted in Francis de Sales, *Introduction to the Devout Life*, trans. John Ryan, Harpers, 1949, chapter 18.

The intimate friendship of St John of the Cross with St Teresa of Avila is well documented, and both of them found strength, inspiration, fulfilment and help on the path to God through their friendship. There are various words for friendship in Greek – one, *hetairos*, means 'associate or comrade' but there is another, *philos*, which means 'the beloved' or 'the dear one'. The Gospel writers used 'philos' when recording Jesus talking to disciples – they were seen as his intimate friends. Real love and intimate friendship is a great gift, to be prized and valued, and it can provide opportunities for growth and development. Basil Hume, Cardinal Archbishop of Westminster, recognizes this when he says:

> Friendship is a way of loving ... When two persons love, they experience in a limited manner in this world what will be their unending delight when one with God in the next ... To love another, whether of the same sex or of a different sex, is to have entered the area of the richest human experience.[3]

The gift of friendship is one of the greatest gifts one person can give to another. No one seriously doubts the value of close friendships. But the question does arise: what are the legitimate forms in which such friendships can be expressed? What are the boundaries between love and friendship? In many cases the two merge into one – genuine, deep, committed friendship (as distinct from casual or social friendships) can be indistinguishable from love. Partly this is the question of the way words are used and different people can use words in different ways. There are two possibilities:

- Person A may say that he or she loves a number of people deeply but is 'in love' with only one,
- Person B may say he has many deep friendships but loves only one person.

[3] Basil Hume, 'Note on Church Teaching Concerning Homosexual People', *Origins* 24 (1995): 767–8.

These two positions are not significantly different, although, perhaps, caution needs to be expressed about the use of 'in love'. This can imply centring one's life on another and if any individual becomes the centre of one's whole life, this can mean losing one's identity and one's individuality.

Intimate friendship should not be problematic (although many consider that such friendships should be exclusive and jealousy quickly creeps in when they are not), but it is when the physical side comes in that problems may arise. A survey conducted in France in 1994 asking what people valued most from a list which included family, children, freedom, independence, friendship, justice, loyalty, employment, love, money, honour, success, sex, patriotism or religion placed friendship firmly at the top of the list with 96 per cent saying friendship was the most important, with family and children in second and third place.[4] Religion was placed last in order of importance.

An element of *eros* may be present in some forms of love which may be absent in friendship. Love can be exciting, it may help a person to 'come alive' and see the world in a new way. However, it is easy to mistake short-term passion for long-term love and commitment. The development of relationships, friendship and love are closely linked. Human beings are made for relationships. This is one of the key meanings of the biblical stories – that human beings are intended to develop 'right relationships' with each other and with God. The problems arise in determining what are 'right relationships' and how they should be manifested.

Although human relationships are essential for personal growth, it may be false to assume that 'falling in love' and a sexual relationship develop individuality – in fact in many cases they may undermine it. It is all too easy for 'falling in love' to be an excuse for 'losing oneself'. A person may well seek to fall in love in order to find happiness or an identity. However, this may be a mistake – it is easy to 'fall in love with love', or to fall for the idea of love rather than the deep commitment that the reality represents.

[4] Cf. Theodore Zeldin, *An Intimate History of Humanity*, Minerva, 1995, p. 333.

Erik Erikson places the achievement of intimacy next after the achievement of identity, and identity as a person is a prerequisite for intimacy. Intimacy also enhances identity so, in the right context, there may be a 'virtuous spiral' of love developing humanity which in turn further develops the ability to love. However, this need not happen and to seek physical intimacy without having an identity of one's own may be a road to nowhere. Some human beings do not really like themselves whilst others like themselves rather too much! Both give rise to problems:

1   Some people may find it almost impossible to believe that another human being can love them – at least the real person that he or she really is when the whole of the outer shell is stripped away. Love is a great compliment to our ego as well as a great gift and, if we are unsure about ourselves, being loved can bolster our self-esteem. It can provide a way of avoiding looking at ourselves by our 'losing ourselves' in our new-found identity as part of a couple. Kierkegaard expresses this well when he talks of a girl who is in despair over having 'lost' her beloved:

> A young girl despairs over love, she despairs over losing the loved one, because he died or became unfaithful. The despair is not declared. No, she despairs over herself. This self of hers, which if it had become 'his' beloved she would have been rid of, or lost, in the most blissful manner – this self, since it is destined to be a self without 'him' is now an embarrassment; this self ... has become, now that 'he' is dead, a loathsome void.[5]

In other words, it is all too easy to take refuge from looking at ourselves by 'losing ourselves' altogether in love of another. This may be a form of 'need' love in which love is being used as a means of running away from one's own identity and, essentially, such love is selfish and self-interested.[6]

[5] Kierkegaard, *Sickness unto Death*, Princeton University Press, p. 50.
[6] C. S. Lewis's *The Four Loves* provides a good analysis of different types of love.

2 On the other hand there are those who like themselves rather too much and who set out to 'love' others as an ego trip or for the pleasure and enjoyment that this brings. Here again the motive for loving may be selfish rather than love being a gift to the beloved which seeks his or her own good whatever one wants oneself.

If one is going to care for another, to be committed to them, to support them and to be interested in the details of their life, then this means taking oneself seriously and getting to know oneself. This is why Jung's talk of integration is so important. One can only love others to the extent that one can first accept oneself and one can only accept oneself if one is at least attempting to know oneself.

To be a friend to someone means having the strength to show this friendship and sometimes to stand against the pressure of others out of loyalty for one's friend. Most so-called friendships are transitory and one 'moves on'. Most people have many acquaintances, but few really close friends whom they can trust whatever happens. If one is fortunate, true friends will endure through the passage of the years. However, one can only be a friend to another if one knows who one is, if one cares enough for oneself to take oneself seriously.

It follows from the above that the person who uses sex as a means of finding identity or as a means for personal pleasure is going to end up disappointed:

> Sex is expected, quite unrealistically, to meet people's needs for meaning, happiness, and pleasure in life.[7]

When sex is used as a means to an end, as a way of trying to 'buy' friendship or as a pleasure with no other meaning, it may well lead to disillusion and, in the end, despair because it is being loaded with expectations that it cannot satisfy. Making love is a gift of oneself to another and should only take place where really deep, committed

[7] Sidney Callahan, 'Sexuality in American Culture', *Reading the Signs of the Times*, ed. Coleman & Sanks, Paulist Press, 1993. The answers to Q.3 in the appendix are significant in this connection.

friendship exists, as this also is a giving of oneself. As the Prophet in Kahlil Gibran's famous work says:

> Then said a rich man, Speak to us of Giving. And he answered:
> You give but little when you give of your possessions.
> It is when you give of yourself that you truly give.
> For what are your possessions but things you keep and guard for fear that you may need them tomorrow?[8]

Of course, many people do not experience the ideal of loving friendship set out here, just as many people do not develop into individuals. But human beings are capable of this degree of relationship, and to be content to settle for anything significantly less may be to be content with second best. Increased knowledge of psychology and human relationships show clearly that human beings need more than simply food and drink – we are creatures made for relationship. Close friendship can make us more fully human and help us to grow as individuals. To turn our backs on such friendship is to deny a central part of our humanity – even if this is done in order to avoid the 'risks' involved in the friendship being given physical expression. A life without friends to challenge and strengthen you is an impoverished life. In genuinely loving others, one will find one's own individuality strengthened and sustained.

Close friendships do not, of course, have to be physically expressed. One of the great strengths of celibacy that is not sufficiently emphasized today is that it can lead the individual to be able to love more widely, to have a greater range of close and intimate friends than might otherwise be possible because a deliberate decision has been taken to forego family or physical relationships which, by their very nature, can tend toward preferential love rather than the non-preferential love called for in the Christian Gospels. Sadly some celibates and others do not see it like this and shun friendships

---

[8] Kahlil Gibran, *The Prophet*, Heinemann, 1926, p. 26.

because of the 'risk' that this might lead on to physical intimacy. C. S. Lewis puts it like this:

> Love anything and your heart will certainly be wrung and possibly broken. If you want to make sure of keeping it intact, you must give your heart to no one, not even to an animal. Wrap it up carefully round with hobbies and little luxuries, avoid all entanglements, lock it up safe in the casket or coffin of your self-ishness. But in that casket – safe, dark, motionless, airless – it will change. It will not be broken, it will become unbreakable, impenetrable, irredeemable. The alternative to tragedy or at least the risk of tragedy, is damnation. The only place outside Heaven where you can be perfectly safe from all the dangers of perturba-tions of love is Hell.
>
> I believe that the most lawless and inordinate loves are less contrary to God's will than a self-invited and self-protective lovelessness.

'Lawless and inordinate' loves are precisely, of course, those loves which conventional morality rejects, and yet these can be life-giving and life-affirming. To close oneself off from close relation-ships because one fears the possibility of any relationship becoming physical is to dehumanize oneself. Even if, against one's better judgement, a relationship is physically expressed, this may do less long-term damage than to refuse to have close friendships at all. One problem we shall have to consider in the next chapter is how a commitment to one intimate friendship in marriage can allow space for other close friendships without jealousy and posses-siveness destroying the first relationship.

Sex Outside Marriage

In a survey of more than 3000 British 16–18-year-olds, most of whom were studying theology and/or philosophy, carried out in conjunction with the writing of this book, 84 per cent said that it was morally right to sleep with someone one loved before one got married. 58 per cent considered that it was also right to sleep with someone even if one was not in a long-term relationship provided it was enjoyable, that the girl did not get pregnant and 'no one got hurt' – in other words, 58 per cent considered recreational sex to be morally acceptable. There was almost no difference between the male and female responses to this question – the figures were 56.6 per cent for girls and 60 per cent for boys. (See pages 231–237 for the detailed figures.)

The survey may, in fact, be misleading, because it does not indicate what individual young people would do themselves – merely what they would consider acceptable if it was to be chosen by others. There is a common attitude of relativism in the sexual field with many people saying, in effect, 'I would not do it, but if that is what they want to do, then it is up to them.' The above statistics do not, therefore, necessarily indicate sexual practice by young people today. What is true without question is that a very large number of young people are sexually active before they are married – many at an age much earlier than their parents would have been. There are various reasons for this but, for the purpose of our discussion, the issue is whether or not this can be considered to be morally right.

The traditional understanding of Natural Law will be unequivocal in condemnation – not simply because sexual activity should be confined to marriage but, even so, must always involve the possibility of procreation and most young people will use contraception. However, as we have seen, the assumptions of the traditional understanding of Natural Law in the sexual field are flawed and cannot provide a sound foundation today. Situation Ethics is of little help in the sexual arena as it will ask whether 'love' is being served – but one of the weaknesses of Situation Ethics is deciding exactly what love entails. At one level the young people involved could say 'of course love is being served', but the issue is not that straightforward. Given that many relationships are short term and that there may be no long term commitment, it is doubtful that Situation Ethics has much application.

The Bible is, despite the attitude of some fundamentalists to sex, of little help. Jesus says nothing about sex before marriage and the prohibitions in the Hebrew Scriptures are, as we have seen, largely due to purity rituals and also to seeing women as property who had to be maintained 'intact' for their future husband. These rules have little application in today's world.

Where, then, might one look for moral guidance in this area? In chapter 13 it was suggested that there were four principles that should underpin any modern approach to sexual morality. These can be summarized as follows:

1 Sexuality is an essential part of human nature. The ability to love and to accept love, to form relationships and to enter into mature, adult sexual bonds depends to a larger extent on the experiences one has as a young child.

2 Any approach to sexual ethics must consider the whole human person and an attempt be made to seek a true understanding of what it is to be fully human.

3 Sex should always be a free act, a gift of intimacy, commitment and trust by one autonomous individual to another. The pleasure involved should come as a by-product of the gift of love and tenderness, never as an end in itself.

4 Lovemaking between two people should be something 'deep' and mysterious. Concentration on the mechanics of the act without an appreciation of its role in the wider relationship misses its true significance.

As we have seen, sex can be destructive where one person uses another not as a human being who is being valued and loved for his or her own sake but rather treats them just in terms of their function. Lovemaking should not simply be an act that produces short-term pleasure but should rather be something deep in which two people are giving of their inmost selves to each other. If this is the

171

case, it can well be a path to human integration and wholeness. On this basis, then, the ideal is that lovemaking should be restricted to relationships where, as a minimum, there is a very high level of trust as well as a willingness by each party to make themselves vulnerable at a deep level. If this is accepted, then to engage in sexual activity when one does not have a strong, long-term commitment to the other person, at least in intimate friendship, may be not just demeaning to oneself but positively damaging.

In making love, it is not like giving the other person an ice cream or a good dinner. It is (or at least it should be) a gift of a fundamental part of our humanity and represents something deep and mysterious. To trivialize it is to demean ourselves and the other person. To be sure, there will be those who reject this and who claim that sex is just for pleasure – essentially no different from eating a good meal or going to the cinema. This type of 'recreational sex' involves no gift of oneself to the other and, to a very large extent, the sexual act is deprived of its meaning. The concentration is then likely to be on performance and the multiple orgasms featured in the pages of *Cosmopolitan* and other magazines. This may well be a misuse of human bodies and can be a slippery slope which can end in damaged individuals. Such an approach may fundamentally damage the human psyche and degrade our value as human beings. If we give ourselves as a gift, in all our vulnerability, tenderness and humanity, to another person, and if this gift is spurned or seen as of little worth, then we are diminished as human beings. If we are valued for no more than our 'sexual function', if our most intimate relations are simply to be characterized by the short-term pleasure they generate, then all the higher human virtues such as love, trust, integrity and commitment will be radically undermined.

If two people are committed to each other, share everything with each other, can trust each other with their inmost selves and are convinced that the depth of their love is such that it will endure the passing of the years and the changes that will take place (even though, of course, they must recognize that they could be mistaken), then it may be morally acceptable to express this intimacy and love in the gift of acts of physical lovemaking. This would be to emphasize the 'unitive' side of lovemaking but to recognize that the procreative side may not then be appropriate, even though the possibility of pregnancy is always present and needs to be considered by the partners involved. However, the dangers also need to be accepted – most relationships do not last. School friendships rarely survive moving away to different communities and are mostly transitory and short-term. This does not mean that they do not appear, at the time, to be very deep, significant and important – but it does mean that great caution is required before one assumes that 'this' relationship will be one that endures or that the commitment that making love symbolizes is a genuine and deep one. Sadly, it often will not be. However, this pessimism does not express an unvarying rule. There can be exceptions and only the individuals concerned can judge – although sometimes the opinions of others can be a helpful guide.

The above view may be rejected. There will be those who say 'Nonsense. All this talk of deep and meaningful relationships is irrelevant. Sex is just good fun. Why should I not go out and have a good evening with my mates, have some drinks and then round the evening off with a girl or boy somewhere? We both will have had a good time, we will take precautions so that she (or I) do not get pregnant and what harm is there? You are just trying to impose an old-fashioned view which I reject.'

It is right to recognize that there is no knock-down argument that can be presented against this position. The dispute rests on a view of the nature of a human being and the extent to which sex is simply a bodily function or whether it is an expression of something much deeper. There can be no simple proof of either position, but any morality which has a religious dimension is going to affirm the irreducible value of each individual. The gift of love is something deep and profound and sex should be an expression of this – to regard it in simply functional terms is to dehumanize and devalue those who take part in it. It is also possible, even with the use of contraception, that pregnancy may result and this possibility cannot be lightly dismissed. Those who do not recognize this position may well have a different view of the importance and value of human beings.

The lack of firm rules will distress some who look for simple solutions, but human beings cannot be fitted into external rule frameworks. Within the Christian tradition, Jesus himself recognized this. Jesus called people to an exceptionally high level of personal responsibility for their own humanity and the humanity of others and to be willing to be accountable to God for the decisions they make. This is not the same as abiding by externally imposed rules. Instead, it emphasizes the quality and depth of the relationship (as well as other relationships that may be affected) as being the vital factors involved in validating sexual relationships, rather than any set of rules or legal framework. This may mean that sex within marriage is morally wrong where the relationship does not justify it (for instance, if it involves the exercise of power or is coercive or in the absence of love), and sex outside marriage may be morally acceptable because it brings life to the couple involved and because it is a genuine mark of the depth of the relationship and expresses the depth and mystery of a shared love.

Conscience and Truth

Although the search for truth about the nature of human beings is important, nevertheless individual conscience must be the final arbiter. A distinction needs to be drawn between 'informed conscience' (which generally means conscience informed and guided by the teachings of a religious group and which would resist individuals exercising their own conscience if it goes against this group) and a decision of conscience taken by an individual after wrestling with the complexities of a situation. In the case of a religious believer such a decision of conscience may seek discernment and involve reflection so that it is taken 'before God'. This latter position does not mean that 'anything goes' provided an individual is content with it. It means, rather, that individuals have to grapple with complex issues for themselves – taking into account the tradition from the past, the search for a perspicuous and truthful understanding of human nature and also undertaking a prolonged process of discernment so that they may properly evaluate their own motivations. Having done this then, in the final analysis, individual conscience in the sexual arena, as elsewhere, must have the final word and the individual must then take responsibility for his or her actions.

Throughout the world, some Catholics are calling for reforms of their Church – they are challenging accepted attitudes to, amongst other things, the imposition of sexual teachings which have little intellectual basis and have been shown to be seriously flawed. The 'We are Church' movement is gaining ground in Australia, Belgium, Brazil, Canada, Chile, France, Italy, Mexico, the Netherlands, Nicaragua, Portugal, Spain, Switzerland, Uruguay and the USA – this movement is calling Catholics and non-Catholics who sympathize with them to sign a declaration which calls for the following:

- A Church of love
- A Church with a new attitude to women
- A Church with a re-evaluated priesthood
- A Church which is mature

In particular, this movement calls for a Church which affirms:

a) The God-given gift of sexuality, but avoids obsession with sexual morality.
b) Everyone; their human rights, sexual orientation, marital status, and those who leave the active priesthood or religious life.
c) That a person's individual conscience is foremost in the making of moral decision, e.g. birth control, freedom of speech, conscientious objection.
d) Commitment to peace, public and domestic non-violence, social, racial and economic justice, the eradication of homelessness and poverty.
e) Preservation of the environment.

This movement has been strongly condemned by the Catholic authorities and, of course in the sexual arena (a), (b) and (c) are particularly threatening to some interpretations of Church teaching (notably (c) with its emphasis on conscience, as this leaves the individual able to wrestle with moral dilemmas and to come to his or her own decision – the Second Vatican Council affirmed this position but in more recent years Church documents have tended to resist the idea that an individual can, in conscience, make decisions that run counter to official Church teaching). Cardinal Basil Hume responded to a December 1996 initiative by the 'We are Church' movement by requiring Catholics to be 'docile' in accepting the teaching of the magisterium. But docility can be an abjuration of personal responsibility and a denial of the autonomy and ability of the individual to make difficult moral choices in complex situations. Any rational account of sexual ethics today must affirm these principles and thus reject 'docile' acceptance of the teachings of any religious grouping.

Summary

Close and intimate friendships are an essential part of human development, and to reject the possibilities they offer is to live an impoverished existence. There is no reason why intimate friendships need to be physically expressed although it may, on some occasions, be appropriate to express particularly deep relationships in this way. However, the depth and mystery involved in the physical gift of oneself to another cannot be over-emphasized and must never be undertaken lightly, without a full recognition of what it represents and the consequences it may have both for oneself and one's partner, and without a recognition of one's other commitments.

SIXTEEN

Marriage

Marriage is a risky endeavour – it is a commitment to another person to stay with them, to share one's life with them, perhaps to create and bring up children through all the changes that may take place. It is easy to 'fall in love', but the seriousness with which marriage needs to be approached is often not appreciated. The dashing young man the lovely young woman marries when she is 23 may turn into the pot-bellied, beer drinking, toenail-picking, boring, unthinking man of 45 who is obsessed with football, television and pictures of pretty young girls – or into the workaholic whose whole life is devoted to work with no time for his wife or other interests in life. The lovely young woman may turn into the introverted housewife, totally obsessed with the tidiness and cleanliness of her house, and lacking all sense of individual identity or worth outside the possessions that she accumulates – or into the successful career woman for whom home and family are an irrelevance. Human beings grow in different ways and the chances are high that, after marriage, two individuals may not grow together but instead grow apart – the divorce rate of approximately 40 per cent in Western society is testimony to this, and the percentage of unhappy marriages is much higher as many stay together for convention or 'for the sake of the children'.

The idea that marriage and a family is the cornerstone of morality has been propagated by certain politicians in the United States and Britain and is often supported by Church groupings – although as we have seen Jesus' teaching did not always accord with this view. The Swedish playwright, Strindberg, denounced the family as 'a retirement home for women wanting an easy life, a prison for men and hell for children'.[1] In saying this, he was expressing pessimism about the family as a place where individuals could develop, but also challenging the accepted wisdom that marriage and family were the highest end for human beings. The antecedents of the emphasis on marriage and the family can be found in Protestantism and also in Hegel and a social view of community which prizes conformity above individuality. However, this pessimism is not necessarily justified. Marriage can be quite the reverse of the above and can provide an opportunity for growth, development and great joy, although Strindberg is right to recognize that it can fall far short of this ideal. In spite of the high divorce rate, most people decide to marry and they do so in the hope that this marriage will provide fulfilment and happiness.

Love sustains and builds human beings as individuals – if it is genuine love. Real love seeks the good of the other, it comes from an individual who has the strength to love freely and this means not being dependent on the other. A love that 'needs' the other, that 'depends' on the other is essentially a selfish, self-seeking and self-centred love and this will be destructive. Love should seek the good of the beloved, it should be a freeing and an enabling love which allows the loved one to develop as an individual. A love which seeks to bind, to constrain, is not love. The woman who tries desperately to 'hang on to her man' may well be showing that she does not truly love him – if she did her question would be 'What is in his best interests no matter how much it hurts me?' The person who cannot truly ask this question, does not truly love.

One cannot hope to build oneself as an individual by 'losing oneself' in love of the other – any attempt to do this is doomed to failure and disappointment. This applies as much in marriage as in other situations. Ibsen's play, *A Doll's House*, gives a terrifying portrayal of what a marriage is like when both parties have lost any

---

[1] Quoted Zeldin, *An Intimate History of Humanity*, p. 364.

sense of autonomy or individuality. In order to be a full marriage, both parties must become individuals in their own right and, in the last scene of *A Doll's House*, this is what Nora recognizes. *The Prophet*, talking of marriage, puts it like this:

> Love one another, but make not a bond of love:
> Let it rather be a moving sea between the shores of your souls.
> Fill each other's cup but drink not from one cup.
> Give one another of your bread but eat not from the same loaf.
> Sing and dance together and be joyous, but let each one of you be alone.
> Even as the strings of the lute are alone though they quiver with the same music.
>
> Give your hearts, but not into each other's keeping.
> For only the hand of Life can contain your hearts.
> And stand together, but not too near together:
> For the pillars of the temple stand apart,
> And the oak tree and the cyprus grow not in each other's shadow.[2]

This is a high ideal of marriage. In practice, how should marriage be regarded? Is it essentially a legal contract or is it primarily a relationship of love? If marriage is essentially a legal contract, then sex within marriage may be essentially a duty, an obligation which goes with the marriage contract. This idea of sex as a duty was the view of the Church in the Middle Ages, but few would seriously maintain this today. If, on the other hand, marriage is essentially a relationship, then sex within marriage is a mark of this relationship. On this basis, sex within marriage is a gift of oneself, a sharing, a trust, an outward sign of something inner and profound. It should unite the two people and bring them closer and may, of course, result in the procreation of children. Sex should not be a way of 'losing

[2] Gibran, *The Prophet*, p. 16.

oneself', or of seeking to find individuality through someone else. If this is the aim then sex will fail and will disappoint. Indeed it may be destructive as it may undermine one's feeling of self-worth.

The Church, throughout its history, has failed to distinguish between 'sex' and 'making love'. Indeed, even if this distinction is accepted, then the Church has concentrated on the sex side and even then has disapproved of it. A distinction must be drawn between 'sex' as a biological act and 'making love' which is something much more profound, indeed full of mystery. The Roman Catholic Church has now, since the Second Vatican Council in 1965, accepted the link between the 'unitive' purpose of sexual activity within marriage and the procreative purpose. However, as we have seen, it is held that these two cannot be separated. It is this that has led to the condemnation by the Catholic Church of sex within marriage unless there is the possibility of pregnancy. Pope Pius XI said that any sexual act within marriage:

... in the exercise of which the act is deprived, by human inter-ference, of its natural power to create life, is an offence against the law of God and of nature and ... those who commit it are guilty of a grave sin.[3]

Artificial means of birth control are thus prohibited. By contrast, the Anglican, Methodist and Uniting Churches emphasize the 'unitive' aspect of sex within marriage – in so doing, they are emphasizing 'making' or 'creating' love between the two parties and they therefore allow the use of contraception so that couples can choose when they wish to have children.

Close friendship is one thing, but marriage should go beyond this – it should be a bringing together of soul mates in love, trust and commitment. If this is the case, then 'making' or 'creating' or 'developing' love within the marriage relationship should be an

---

[3] *Casti Connubii* 56. This language is directly echoed in Paul VI's *Humanae Vitae* 11.

essential part of lovemaking. It should unite the couple and, in the intimacy of the bedroom, should enable them to develop trust and commitment to each other in times of joy and tenderness. It should also, and this is by no means the least important element, improve communication. In the tender moments after lovemaking, the couple may be able to communicate in a way that at other times they might find more difficult.

Marriage and the relationship and love it represents is not a one-off affair, attested at the marriage service and then secure for life. It is a commitment to fidelity, to sexual exclusivity and to a union of two people in love, and this love needs to be developed, preserved and fostered. Marriage is not an achievement, it is a task for life – a task of building and maintaining love and intimacy and concern for the other. If this occurs, marriage can and should be an enriching, strengthening experience which builds individuality rather than undermines it, and in which both parties benefit from the love and insights of the other. At its best, a true marriage is something precious and wonderful, but such marriages do not occur frequently, nor do they occur without effort on behalf of both parties to keep the love fresh and alive and to maintain the open communication that is essential for trust to be built and retained.

The importance of lovemaking within marriage cannot be over-estimated, and it can be seen as a joy and a pleasure, uniting two people and bringing them closer together in mutual trust. However, this does not always happen – marriages grow cold, and whilst one person may want to be physically close, the other may not. It is all too easy for a couple who were once close to drift apart. Often problems within a marriage in the sexual arena are a sign of some more fundamental problem in the relationship and one cannot resolve the sexual difficulties without addressing the problems that give rise to them. In November 1996, a husband, signing himself 'Frustrated in New Orleans' wrote to Ann Landers, the American agony aunt, saying:

So far as I know, marriage vows do not include a vow of celibacy
... So why isn't sex considered part of marriage maintenance?
She doesn't want sex? Too bad. I don't want to get up Saturday
morning and clean the storm drains, but I do it anyway.

This view clearly sees sex as a duty – one which the woman should
perform just as the man has to clear the drains. When this letter was
published, it provoked a tidal wave of letters from across the United
States – men and women who expressed the same sentiments. The
demand is for the woman or man in a relationship to 'do their duty'
– there are clear echoes here of the Middle Ages idea of sex as a duty.
However, to demand sexual access is, again, to treat the partner as an
object. It is a form of abuse. If the 'unwilling' partner is advised to
'do their duty' out of love for the other person, it is all too easy for
the spontaneity and intimacy involved in lovemaking to be undermined. In this case, if there is any sexual activity it may be purely
functional and a denial rather than an affirmation of love. As one
respondent to Ann Landers, who had advised on how to increase
sexual interest in a marriage, said:

> Your advice is lousy. My wife is an icicle. I have tried foreplay,
> five-play, six-play, forget it. In the middle of everything, she says,
> 'I hope you're enjoying this. It isn't doing a darn thing for me.'

This pointedly expresses the problems that arise in marriage – it is
not easy to keep a marriage 'fresh', to maintain genuine intimacy
and sharing. The sexual aspect of marriage can become boring,
routine and a duty – if it exists at all. Such boredom may well reflect
a wider boredom and lack of communication in the marriage as
a whole.

As we have seen, in the Middle Ages, sex within marriage was
not written about in terms of developing love – instead it represented a duty within marriage, a duty which the woman was bound
to pay to her husband. This idea has, fortunately, largely been
relegated to the past. However, it may still be that duty within a

marriage relationship and a new trust and intimacy found outside it may sometimes create tension. Duty and the love that may or may not be present after some years of marriage may call the individual to be obedient to its commands, yet new friendships may lead an individual to question this sense of duty. These tensions are genuine and are part of being human – they are not easily resolved.

Theodore Zeldin argues that intimacy has meant different things over the years:[4]

1 It was originally concerned with space and objects, an intimate room or souvenirs such as a lock of hair which were cherished as almost magical tokens. Within marriage, intimacy meant domesticity, friends expressed their intimacy by falling into each other's arms and lying close together. In many countries, touch and embrace remain the signs of intimacy between friends.

2 The Romantic movement considered this to be inadequate and invented a revolutionary new kind of intimacy because it claimed that men and women could, through sexual intercourse, enjoy the kind of intimacy which ancient philosophers maintained was reserved for men only. Previously a man was meant to fall in love with a woman and then to give respectability to his passion by marrying her – only after this was sex permissible. The Romantics, according to Zeldin, maintained that sex and being 'in love' alone was all that was required and through this the two people merged into one. Sex was held to be the great guarantor of harmony.

3 Today a third kind of intimacy has emerged, an intimacy of persons – whole, developing individuals. As Zeldin puts it:

Instead of constantly asking each other 'Are you still besotted with me?' the question has become 'Do you still interest me, stimulate me, help me, comfort me and care for me as I change and grow and do I do the same thing for you?'

[4] Zeldin, *An Intimate History of Humanity*, pp. 324–6.

This intimacy is a partnership in the search for truth, enabling each to see the world twice over, through the other's eyes as well as one's own. The individuals are not the same, but their differences enable each other to explore, together, what they could not achieve alone.

The above three types of intimacy are not exclusive, and the challenge today is to integrate them. This points to a need for a very high ideal of marriage based on mutual relationship and companionship. The problems are obvious – close and intimate friendships may well exist outside marriage and yet these are often viewed with suspicion by the marriage partner who may well feel the need for an exclusive love that runs counter to such relationships. A marriage based on close companionship is obviously the right ideal at which to aim, but

- Such marriage relationships are not always going to continue at the level that existed when the marriage occurred.
- Even if the relationship continues at the same level, this may no longer satisfy one or the other party to a marriage – this is one of the challenges of marriage.
- Any one relationship is unlikely to be fully satisfying and to meet all the needs of an individual for the whole of his or her life.

If the third point is accepted, then the very idea of marriage as presently conceived by many may have to be reconsidered. This can be done both by returning to a broader view of relationships from the past and also by meeting the challenge of the future which stems from a greater appreciation of human sexual natures. It is only relatively recently that the 'nuclear family' or the 'nuclear couple' has been expected to carry all the relational needs of each partner. This has developed in part due to family ties being undermined by the ease of travel and also by extra-familial friendships. The impact of the Romantic movement also had an effect here, and still does, in so far as people expect marriage to answer all their relational needs.

The challenge that human beings now face is to develop new models of relationships which will affirm the need for intimacy with more than one person but will also retain the value of marriage as a warm, secure setting in which the two partners can find companionship, trust and passion and in which any children can develop and grow. Present models find great difficulty in integrating these positions, which results in a new intimacy found by one partner in a marriage often leading to a breakdown of the existing marriage. One of the remedies against this, as well as one of the cornerstones of a successful marriage, may be a high level of communication between the parties. When this is present, other friendships can then be understood and seen as non-threatening. Once communication declines, however, then the marriage as a whole may be under threat.

Throughout this chapter, reference has been made to marriage – but this term needs definition. Is a marriage one that takes place only in church or some other religious building or one that is legally valid (say, for instance, being performed at a registry office), or does it extend to include cohabitation? The boundary lines are not clear-cut, and a couple who are committed to each other and who live together may be in a relationship which, in every respect except legality or religious validity, constitutes a marriage. We have previously seen that Christians have not always regarded a marriage as primarily a religious rite and not all Christians regard it as a sacrament. The key issue may be the intention with which two people live together and the commitments they make to each other. Divorce or separation may be a breach of commitments made and may, essentially, be seen as a failure because they represent breaches of vows made. Not all cohabiting couples make such commitments to each other but if they are made then a breakdown of a relationship may be considered to be more serious and hurtful. Such vows or commitments, whether in marriage or as part of cohabitation, may be particularly appropriate where there is a possibility of children, as any break-up of the relationship then affects not just the couple but the children as well.

It may, therefore, be that the boundary lines between marriage and cohabitation are less clear than in the past and that the intentions of the couple are more important morally than the outward or legal form. The issue of divorce or separation will be dealt with in the next chapter.

Summary

Marriage is a risky endeavour in which two people commit themselves to each other for life with no certainty that the existing passion will endure or that they will continue to challenge and help each other develop over the years. It is a task for life, not an achievement at the wedding service. At its best, marriage can provide a setting for the highest form of friendship, companionship, trust, communication and love and a secure and stable place in which children can be nurtured. Lovemaking within marriage should be an expression of the relationship which 'builds' strengthens and creates love – but it can also deteriorate into a purely physical act which can verge on abuse. Marriage should be a commitment by and a gift of two people to each other and should never be based on need or possession – it should give expression to a freeing and enabling love and should seek to bring life, freshness and growth to both partners.

SEVENTEEN

Adultery and Divorce

Adultery

Adultery is clearly condemned by both the Old and New Testaments.[1] This is partly due to it being seen as a violation of property rights (cf. pp. 21 and 29). Both men and women were able to commit adultery but only women could commit adultery against their husbands because they were breaching his property rights over her. It was accepted that a man had sole rights over his wife's body and adultery was punishable by death. Thus:

> If a man is found lying with the wife of another man, both of them shall die, the man who lay with the woman and the woman. (Deuteronomy 22:22)

It is important in any modern account of sexuality to consider the issue of adultery and how it should be approached. The simple reaction is to condemn it under all circumstances. Such a deontological approach would be taken by supporters of Natural Law which would condemn adultery as 'intrinsically evil' in any situation. However, the position may not be as simple as that,[2] and traditional

---

[1] There are 18 references in the OT to adultery, compared to more than 50 to circumcision, which was regarded as of far more importance as it was one of the signs of communal identity for the Israelites.

[2] Films such as *The Bridges of Maddison County*, *Shirley Valentine* and books such as D. H. Lawrence's *Lady Chatterley's Lover* provide examples of alternative perspectives on adultery.

Natural Law approaches to sexual morality have been seen to rest on questionable premises.

There may be many reasons for a man or woman committing adultery. A middle-aged person may face a mid-life crisis. He or she may feel the onset of age and feel no longer attractive. The response may then be to try to perpetuate youth by entering into a relationship with someone considerably younger. Such relationships can be flattering to the ego and can also bring a sense of excitement. Part of this may be due to the illicit and clandestine nature of the relationship, which may add a thrilling and unpredictable element to a life that may otherwise seem set in the hamster wheel of routine. A new relationship may also seem to offer the promise of enjoyment and fulfilment which has been found to be wanting in the existing relationship. And, of course, an imbalance of physical intimacy within marriage may also lead a person to an extra-marital sexual relationship. A further reason for adultery may be the increased modern expectations laid on marriage – expectations which in many cases cannot be fulfilled. 'Affairs' are common, with more than 60 per cent of males admitting having had adulterous relationships and the figure for women being only slightly lower.

Carl Jung took seriously the different ages of human beings ranging from the passion of early adulthood to the calmer but no more complex waters of middle age. As he says:

> We cannot live in the afternoon of life according to the programme of life's morning.[3]

As Ferder and Heagle put it, the later stages of life involve a shift from orienting ourselves towards the outer world to an inner search:

> … we can say that the first half of life – the morning – is primarily orientated toward relating to the outer world. It is

---

[3] Carl Jung, *Modern Man in Search of a Soul*, quoted in *Your Second Self*, Ferder & Heagle, p. 121.

concerned with establishing our ego-identity, our social roles, our place in the scheme of things. The second half of life – the afternoon – is orientated more towards the inner world ... it redirects our energies to issues of interiority, generativity, and intimacy ... we are challenged to rediscover that we are human *beings* before we are human *doings*.[4]

One feature that may well come to the fore in the later years of a person's life is the need for genuine and deep intimacy – this need may never previously have been recognized even by those who have been married and have had an apparently good sex life. Genuine intimacy may have eluded them and a depth of love and of relationship may emerge with another person which is truly life-giving.

St Augustine wrote, 'In the evening of our lives we will all be judged by love'. What may be of ultimate value to us is to be fully understood, warts and all, and to be loved and accepted as we are. Problems arise when this intimacy occurs with someone to whom a person may not be married. This intimacy may, seemingly naturally, become sexual – expressing physically a great love, commitment and trust. The moral issues here are whether:

a) A deep, intimate but non-physical relationship should exist if one is married to someone else, and

b) Whether such a relationship can be given physical expression.

It is here that genuine human dilemmas may arise, because existing ideas of marriage cannot accommodate multiple intimate friendships.

There seems little doubt that (a) is acceptable – to deny this would be to deny a human being who is married close friendships with anyone except for the marriage partner. The real moral problems arise with (b). Obviously (b) is not the ideal but whether it is always morally unacceptable may be debatable. Take two examples:

[4] Fran Ferder & John Heagle, *Your Sexual Self*, Ave Maria Press, 1992, p. 122.

1   A woman is married to a man who drinks heavily and beats her, who shows little interest in her and she is left at home with two young children. She feels a responsibility to them and also considers that she must maintain the marriage in their interests. In this case, if she finds another person who is tender and understanding, who cares for her and who shows gentleness and love then to express this love physically may well enable her to keep the marriage together as without this outlet her grim situation might be simply intolerable.

2   A husband has come from a background in which he has had difficulty coming to terms with his sexuality and is not close to his wife (possibly for reasons connected with his childhood of the sort set out in chapter 10). The couple may have married young and never have communicated well, and may have grown apart. Assume that the couple's sex life verges on the non-existent and that he often feels humiliated by her, yet still cares for and loves her. If, in this situation, the man has an affair even though he intends to remain married, then, although this is not ideal by the standards of a close marriage, it may further his humanity rather than letting him continue to be 'enclosed' and shut off from close human relationships.

Many alternative scenarios can be painted in which, for one reason or another and not necessarily due to the fault of either party, the marriage relationship has cooled. It may even be that the marriage is still an expression of love, but a deeper or different relationship may be found which meets the human needs of one of the parties which has not previously been acknowledged. Talk of such 'needs' may seem to imply weakness but all human beings do have needs, as Jung recognized, and if they are not met within the marriage then other relationships may then develop which may not necessarily be evil or wicked. Clearly the preferable course would be for the marriage to be helped to develop and grow – possibly with the assistance of counselling services, but this may not always be possible.

We have seen in the previous section that coming to human wholeness, psychologically and spiritually, is part of the journey everyone has to undertake. This journey necessarily involves relationships with others, yet forming these relationships may be difficult. For many, their sexual development can be stunted and distorted by childhood events. Sometimes, an 'affair' can actually aid this process in a way in which marriage has never done. Also, some people who are married may come to find that their marriage partner does not provide the opportunity for close, intimate friendship which they may (rightly or wrongly) see as vital to their development as human beings. The film *Shirley Valentine* portrays this well, with Shirley locked into a humdrum relationship in which she verges on despair. Her eventual and short-lived 'affair' brought her to see and value the world in a new way – in a genuine sense she came 'alive', having been locked into a mediocre existence from which there seemed no escape. Natural Law will condemn her action as evil, but those with a less absolutist view of ethics may see arguments in favour of it being seen as morally justifiable in the circumstances.

If one believes in the need for full human development (in the case of those with a religious perspective they may well add here 'before God'), then a rejection of genuine and deep intimacy for the sake of 'keeping the rules' or maintaining a quasi-legal marriage obligation may, in certain circumstances, be to choose death rather than life. It may, in fact, stunt a human being's psychological and spiritual growth. Intimacy does not, of course, have to be expressed physically, but there may be circumstances when it seems an appropriate expression of a deep relationship and the issue is then whether the final word is expressed by generally accepted moral rules or whether there can be exceptions. As Blake said:

> If moral virtue was Christianity,
> Christ's pretensions were all vanity.

Blake may be saying here that living a life of love, of finding life rather than death through an openness to the depth and profundity of human relationships by being open to love, may be closer to what God requires than keeping a set of rules.

The Catholic psychiatrist Jack Dominian sees adultery in a different light from that taken by his Church:

> Adultery can now be seen as a symptom in a marriage when the minimum needs of one or two people are not being met. This concept of the minimum needs evokes deep opposition from those who think only in terms of an abstract concept of the common good and ignore the reality of individual needs ... adultery is a cry for help arising from the depths of a tottering relationship.
>
> Adultery is either a cry for help or the sign of the death or non-existence of a relationship. Its significance has little to do with the enjoyment of an illicit pleasure outside the matrimonial bond ...
>
> ... the Christian response to adultery must be ... to examine the quality of a marriage: to find out whether a marriage really exists or not and if it does, however minimally, to help the couple in every way to restore their marital relationship.[5]

In the 1996–7 survey of young people in Britain, 52 per cent considered that adultery could never be morally justified (see appendix). This is to take a deontological approach and to maintain that adultery is always, under any circumstances, morally evil. Situation Ethics, by contrast, will demand that each situation should be looked on based at its merits and will resist any idea of absolute rules. However, there are dangers in appealing to consequences or particular situations to justify adultery. Once exceptional circumstances are allowed then the question arises, in individual cases, exactly what the 'exceptional circumstances' might be. The danger is then of a slippery slope which would allow lack of fidelity to the marriage partner to occur relatively easily, undermining the

---

[5] Jack Dominian, *The Church and the Sexual Revolution*, pp. 39–41.

marriage and not forcing the parties involved to confront their difficulties and to try to resolve them. The importance of trust and fidelity in marriage cannot be underestimated, and it is linked, as was made clear in the previous chapter, with good communication. Once 'secrets' creep in between marriage partners, once communication and trust breaks down then the marriage is heading for stormy waters – if not for the rocks.

It is too easy to say that the person who commits adultery is necessarily the only guilty party – if, indeed, it is right to talk of 'guilt' at all, which may be debatable. As Helmut Thielicke puts it:

> Even if the legally definable guilt of the one partner is clearly established, say on the grounds of wilful desertion of the family or proved permanent adultery, there is still the ethical, and therefore largely non-judiciable, question whether this proved desertion of the marriage may be a reaction to a deeper insufficiency in the other partner – his incapability to be erotically attractive or to create a homelike atmosphere or to provide certain non rational conditions for communication ... as a general rule, the person who looks deeper will find that in every case both are involved in the guilt of a broken marriage and that the outwardly innocent or less guilty party is more at fault in the breakdown of the marriage than the other.[6]

Roger Ormerod, a judge of the Family Division of the British High Court of Justice who died in 1996 said:

> The forensic process is much too clumsy a tool for dissecting the complex interactions which go on all the time in a family. Shares in responsibility for breakdowns of marriages cannot be properly assessed without a meticulous examination and understanding of the characters and personalities of the spouses concerned, and the more thorough the investigation, the more the shares will, in most cases, approach equality.

[6] Thielicke, *The Ethics of Sex*, p. 171.

St Paul condemned a long list of sins but he did not single out sexual sins for any graver mention than others. Peter Mullen, an Anglican priest who resigned for committing adultery with a parishioner, wrote as follows:

> ... fornication is sinful all right, and no two ways about it. But ... why is it one never hears of anyone thrown out of the Mothers' Union for backbiting or rejected from General Synod for party-strife?[7]

What Mullen is challenging is the idea that sexual sins should be treated more seriously than any others. However, he fails to take into account two things: firstly the fact that adultery may be far more damaging because of its significance for the humanity of the people involved, and secondly because of the potential damage inflicted by the person committing adultery on his or her partner and possible children. Actions cannot be isolated from their effects on others and whilst, in themselves, such actions could be justifiable in some cases, the hurt they may cause must not be underestimated. Too few people entering on a path that may lead to adultery think seriously about the damaging effect this may have on the wife or husband. This is too often forgotten, particularly when the parties reassure themselves that 'no one will know'. Such an attitude avoids confronting the moral ambiguities – something that is morally wrong is wrong whether or not anyone knows about it.

Having said this, human relationships are complicated and their complexity cannot be measured or dealt with solely by appeal to simple rules. Jesus rejected the rule-based approach of the Torah and called people to wrestle with the need to become fully human and the need to love in the particular situations in which they found themselves. His approach constantly led to criticism or rejection by the established institutions of his day, but he saw human beings having a higher call than keeping the rules. They were called to live in

---

[7] *The Independent*, 25 September, 1996.

relationship with God, to live, as Luther put it, *Coram Deo* (in the heart of God), and to wrestle with what this means in the ambiguities of everyday life. The same must surely apply in the sexual arena today. This most certainly does not mean that 'anything goes' – instead it is to affirm anew the traditional understanding of the depth, mystery and importance of sexual relationships and to only see these being appropriate as part of a deep, permanent commitment of love. Whether only one such 'deep, permanent commitment' is possible in a human life is precisely where the problems arise.

Divorce

The expectations of marriage today are higher than ever in the past – not least because life-expectancy is far longer than even a hundred years ago. Whereas in previous centuries parents might well die before the children reached the age of 20, now adults in the West can expect to live to 70, 80 or even longer. There will thus be a very long period in which husband and wife are together without the children. The expectations in terms of mutual companionship, sharing and growing together as human beings are far greater than earlier generations could imagine. What is more, the main occupation of a woman is no longer child bearing and child rearing. Many women will have their own careers, hobbies and interests and there will be full equality between the man and the woman. It is not surprising that, in these radically changed circumstances, the likelihood of marriage breakdown is increased.

Muriel Porter points out a significant shift in the ordering of the purposes of marriage. She writes:

> One of the immediate outcomes of the Reformation debate about marriage was a reconsideration of the grounds for divorce. From the earliest days of the Reformation, there can be traced a minority view that the first 'cause' of marriage was companionship ('mutual society') rather than either procreation, which had always dominated traditional Christian theology, or 'remedy'.

The Strasbourg reformer, Martin Bucer ... took issue with Cranmer's marriage service published in the first Book of Common Prayer of 1549. Bucer argued that priority should have been given to mutual society.[8]

This is important, because Cranmer's Book of Common Prayer has always been the cornerstone of the Anglican liturgy in all the many provinces of the Anglican Communion. Cranmer followed the traditional Christian position, as well as the position of Aquinas, in saying that procreation was the primary purpose of marriage. If this is challenged, then the whole basis for marriage may need to be reconsidered. Most contemporary Anglican marriage services now side with Bucer and accept that mutual society is the main focus of marriage. This is significant, as companionship rests on love and if this dies then it may be held that the whole basis on which the marriage is built may have collapsed as well. Unless marriage is to be seen in contractual terms, as if the two parties had entered into a quasi-legally binding contract that had to remain in force until death, then it may be held that just as love and intimacy of relationship may come to an end, so may marriage.

However, it is not as simple as this – for instance if a couple marry and there are young children, then for one person just to decide that 'love has died' and therefore the marriage is at an end does not take into account the commitment to the other partner and to children. The importance of a stable, loving home in which children can develop cannot be overestimated. However, the fact that a couple stay together after the marriage has effectively died is certainly no guarantee of the presence of such a home.

Jesus' command apparently forbidding divorce has already been dealt with and this appears to forbid divorce entirely (cf. pp. 39–40). However, Bernard Hoose points out that this may well not have been the case if the Hebrew word *porneia* is understood to refer to fornication,[9] and if this is read (as is common in the Hebrew

[8] Porter, *Sex, Marriage and the Church*, Dove, p. 104.
[9] Hoose, 'Imitating Jesus and Allowing Divorce'.

Scriptures) as referring to those who follow other Gods.[10] In this case, Jesus may have intended to allow for a genuine exception to the general rule against divorce – permitting it if the other partner in a marriage made it difficult to grow in holiness together. On this basis, a modern approach could be adopted which would allow divorce if the marriage, instead of building up the couple and enabling them to grow as human beings, was instead seen as destructive and dehumanizing.

Adultery has historically been accepted as the only grounds for divorce (cf. p. 38), although there tends to have been an imbalance between male and female adultery. Female adultery has traditionally been regarded and treated far more harshly than male adultery. The reason is easy to see – female adultery may result in children who are not then the children of the husband and the husband's property rights and his rights of descent are therefore infringed. In Victorian times, many men in Britain had mistresses and this was generally accepted, but it was unacceptable socially for women to have lovers. The imbalance which started in the Old Testament has continued up until the present day. Divorce has been frowned on particularly because it meant the break-up of the family unit, and in Protestant Christianity in particular, the family has been regarded as of central importance.

If it is argued that adultery is a ground for divorce because it undermines the main purpose of marriage when this is seen as procreation, then today it may alternatively be argued that if the marriage has failed because of a lack of love, intimacy, communication or companionship between the parties, then this may also be a ground for divorce. This latter view has led to the modern view of divorce based on an 'irretrievable breakdown of marriage'.

Until recently, marriage was seen as conferring rights over the wife to the husband and the ideal of a mutual loving relationship had little part to play in a theological understanding of marriage. Today, Churches make pronouncements as though they have always

[10] E.g. Deuteronomy 31:16; Ezra 10:10–11.

considered this to be central, but this is in fact far from the case. It was only in 1891 that Anglican Canon Law no longer allowed husbands to 'moderately correct' their wives. The idea of a husband having total rights over the woman's body extended to him being allowed to beat her, and the Church raised no difficulty with this. It was not until 1937 that British Law recognized wife-beating as a possible cause of divorce. This point is significant as it indicates the way in which human understanding develops over time.

The Catholic Church's prohibition on divorce and remarriage has, from the time of the early Church Fathers, been based on Ephesians 5:21–28 – in other words, a man's love for his wife is modelled on Christ's love for the Church. However, this original theological vision has become overlaid with emphasis on the legal status of marriage under Canon Law. It is one thing to exhort people to behave well as St Paul does in this passage, it is quite another to rule out the possibility of failure and a new start.[11] Kevin Kelly rejects the idea of marriage as an indissoluble, legal bond and instead bases his view of marriage on the couple's love for each other. He sees the aim of marriage as maintaining the quality of the relationship between the couple, but he also accepts that a marriage can die and that a second marriage may then be morally right.[12] Kelly is, therefore, close to the position taken by the Orthodox Church but some way from his own (Catholic) Church's official position.

The idea of the development of Christian doctrine has already been discussed in chapter 1 and this can be seen in attitudes to divorce within the Anglican Communion. The Anglican Church, unlike the Roman Catholic, delegates a great deal of power in such matters to local provinces. The 'glue' which binds the Anglican Communion together is much thinner than the tight control over liturgy, theology and doctrine maintained by the Roman Catholic hierarchy. Today, the main factors in the Anglican glue are the common past history which is based on the Book of Common

[11] I am indebted here to the insights of Sr Catherine Cowley.
[12] Kevin Kelly, *Divorce and Second Marriage: Facing the Challenge*, Collins, 1982.

Prayer and the ten-yearly meetings of all Anglican primates known as the Lambeth Conference. The 1988 Lambeth Conference suggested that the innocent party in a divorce should be allowed to remarry and also to partake in the Eucharist. Previously a second marriage had been rejected and divorced people were not allowed to take Communion. It was only in 1966 that a report of the Church of England rejected the old idea of divorce being based on the fault of one party and substituted the idea of the irreversible breakdown of a marriage.[13] This recognizes the complexity of marriage breakdown and that such breakdown has many and varied causes. Divorce is rarely the fault of one party alone and many complex factors may contribute to the breakdown.

By 1971, the Church of England was recommending remarriage in Church of divorced people, although even today practice varies with different Church of England dioceses and different priests adopting varying positions. This diversity of practice is one of the strengths and one of the weaknesses of the Anglican communion. It allows for diverse interpretations as the Church tries to seek the mind of God in today's world, although also means that there is no single, consistent view. It can be contrasted with the more rigid, because more centrally controlled, Roman Catholic practice. This, in turn, has strengths as well as weaknesses – it ensures a world-wide uniformity of practice but it can also be rigid and slow to respond to change.

The issue is not whether divorce is desirable – clearly it is not. The issue is whether two people who have loved each other deeply enough to have wanted to share the whole of their lives together may come to the conclusion that their marriage has failed; that their relationship has irretrievably broken down and that it is preferable to start again. No one would ever take such a decision easily: it is full of pain and distress and is never easy for either party, nor for the children and others who may be affected. Indeed divorce is regarded as one of the most traumatic events that can happen to a person and

[13] *Putting Asunder: a Divorce Law for Contemporary Society*, SPCK, 1966.

everyone would prefer to remain in a loving, intimate marriage. When this is not possible, then, after a period of reflection and thought, it may be that the most loving thing to do can be to part – hopefully maintaining links of respect and friendship and trying to understand the viewpoint of the other rather than each person internalizing his or her own hurt and lashing out in anger at the 'guilty' party. Sometimes a breakdown of marriage may be no one's 'fault' – human beings grow in different ways and may simply grow apart so that they can no longer provide the companionship, solace and challenge to each other that any real relationship should involve. When this happens, to add to the burden of the parties involved by emphasizing their guilt rather than by helping them to look to their futures, to come to terms with their past mistakes and to learn from them would certainly not have been Jesus' way of proceeding.

Summary

Those entering marriage or committing themselves permanently to each other outside the bounds of formal marriage should do so in the expectation that it will be for life and there will be only one sexual partner. Adultery means a breach of trust and radically undermines the marriage relationship, although it may be a sign of problems in a marriage rather than a cause. Whether adultery can ever be morally justified by exceptional circumstances is a question that cannot be simply answered as it depends on whether one considers there are absolute moral rules or whether a consequentialist view of ethics is adopted. Certainly, the damage and hurt it may inflict on the marriage partner(s) and on children are likely to be enormous.

The central issue may be whether marriage is seen in contractual terms as something which must be maintained no matter what the cost, or whether the time can come for a fresh start. A marriage can fail and can 'drag down' the couple involved – in this case it may be right to bring it to an end. No one would choose this as an ideal, but when it happens it should be met with understanding, not least by both parties in the relationship who may well be badly hurt.

EIGHTEEN

Homosexuality

The word 'homosexual' was first used as a medical term in 1882 – 'homo' means 'same', and the word can cover both male and female inclination to the same sex. Many people with such orientations prefer the word 'gay'. The term 'lesbian' applies only to women and comes from the poetry of Sappho who lived around 500 BC on the Aegean island of Lesbos.

It is now clear that human beings are not simply either heterosexual or homosexual. The American researcher Kinsey, writing particularly on males, says that human beings:

> do not represent two discrete populations, heterosexual and homosexual. The world is not divided into sheep and goats. Not all things are black nor are all things white ... The living world is a continuum in each and every one of its aspects. The sooner we learn this concerning sexual behaviour the sooner we shall reach a sound understanding of the realities of sex.[1]

Kinsey's extensive surveys indicate that less than 50 per cent of males and less than 60 per cent of females reported that they were exclusively heterosexual. The fact that someone is attracted to a member of the same sex or even has a physical relationship with that person does not mean that they are exclusively homosexual. About 4 per cent of the male population are exclusively homosexual and a smaller percentage are exclusively lesbian (in this book I use

[1] A. C. Kinsey, *Sexual Behaviour in the Human Male*, 1953, p. 470.

'homosexual' to refer to male homosexuals and 'lesbian' to refer to female homosexuals solely to simplify differentiation).

There are two chromosomes which determine gender: the large X chromosome and the smaller Y chromosome. The 'default option' for human gender is female and a Y chromosome needs to be inherited for a male to develop. So an X chromosome inherited from both parents (XX) produces a female, whilst an X and Y (XY) produces a male. There are a variety of other combinations that can occur as abnormalities. It is important, however, to separate:

- **Gender** – which is undoubtedly inherited based on the chromosomes (XX or XY), and
- **Sexual orientation** – the origins of which are still not clear, although current thinking in psychology and genetics tends to the view that it is due to both genetic and early neuro-physical factors.

It may be that stress or other factors in the mother may cause an alteration of the hormonal balance which will affect the sexual tendencies of the child. It may also be – although this seems less likely – that homosexual inclination is largely due to experiences in the early years of sexual development, including the different ways in which the child learns to relate to mother and father, and, consequently, to other women and other men.

As in so many areas related to sexuality, three factors have determined modern attitudes to homosexuality – these are the Hebrew Scriptures, the New Testament writings, and the Natural Law tradition coming from Plato and Aristotle. These will be dealt with in turn.

a) The Old Testament

The Bible portrays homosexuality as a freely chosen activity – there is no suggestion or discussion of the idea that inclination towards a member of the same sex may be a matter of genetics or background or the nature of the individual concerned. This is an important distinction to which we shall return. The lack of awareness of modern knowledge about sexuality radically undermines the usefulness of the biblical material as a guide to conduct today.

It is worth noting that there is no condemnation of lesbian behaviour in either the Old or New Testament (other than in Romans 1:26 where 'unnatural acts' between women are referred to) and, indeed, almost all rules and laws drawn up since have been directed at male rather than female homosexual behaviour. The biblical approach to male homosexuality seems to be clear-cut – it is condemned everywhere it is referred to. The condemnations are, moreover, unambiguous. For instance:

> You shall not lie with a male as with a woman; it is an abomination.[2]

The 'Holiness Code' lays down the death penalty for sexual intercourse between males.[3] In Deuteronomy there is a prohibition against Temple prostitution, including male prostitution, and the use of money from prostitution to pay religious dues is forbidden.[4] It may well be that male prostitution was a mainly money-making activity which was given a pagan religious 'cloak' to make it respectable. If this is the case, it is not surprising that it should have been condemned by Israel's religious leaders. The context of such statements need to be noted. For instance, the above commandment is part of a list of acts which are condemned which includes a condemnation of a man having sex with a woman whilst she has a period. Few people today would consider that any moral problem arises with this – the question then becomes why homosexuality should be treated in a different light to a husband and wife making love in this way.

Some of the Hebraic stories which are claimed to bear on the

[2] Leviticus 18:22; 20:13.
[3] Leviticus 20:13.
[4] Deuteronomy 23:17–18.

debate about homosexuality have already been examined. The distance between the time of the biblical writers and the situation today is immense and it simply is not possible to translate prohibitions from the one time to our own. For instance, polygamy is accepted in the Hebrew Scriptures,[5] yet some time before the coming of Jesus it was replaced by monogamy. As Gareth Moore, OP points out, there is no condemnation in the Old Testament of lesbian behaviour – this is because the condemnation of homosexuality was due to a man taking a subservient role (as a woman) and therefore demeaning himself.[6] The condemnation is of a man lying with a man 'as if with a woman'.[7] This did not happen when a woman slept with another woman. On this basis, if women are considered equal to men then the basis for the condemnation of homosexuality disappears.

It is necessary to separate the sometimes unquestioned acceptance of ideas such as disapproval of homosexual or lesbian relationships from the view that this is necessarily what God – if one believes in God – commands. It is too simple to think that prevailing preconceptions accurately reflect the divine will. The culture within which each individual grows up impresses on him or her taboos and ethical norms which generally go unquestioned until the individual is old enough to become a philosopher and to think for themselves. It is too easy to assume that what we have been brought up to think must be right. Throughout the history of Christianity, the assumption that prevailing norms accurately reflect what God wishes tends to have been accepted by many. It justified, for instance, the Church accepting slavery; accepting the feudal structure of society; accepting that women were inferior to men or accepting that, in marriage, men had sole rights over the bodies of their wives.

William Countryman maintains that the Old Testament prohibition against homosexuality is part of the Israelite prohibition

[5] Deuteronomy 21:15–17.
[6] Moore, *The Body in Context*, p. 39.
[7] Leviticus 20:13.

against mixing different kinds of things. Each thing is held to have a particular nature and one must not bring together two natures. Thus there is a prohibition on:

- Using two materials together to make a garment.[8]
- Having two different types of plant in the same field.
- Different domestic animals mating (for instance a donkey and a horse to produce a mule).
- A human being mating with an animal.[9]
- A man assuming a woman's role. The man who takes on a woman's role is a combination of male and female and is therefore unclean. The same point is made in the prohibition against a man dressing as a woman.[10]

The rejection of homosexuality is, thus, part of a much wider prohibition against 'impurity'. The need to maintain purity was central to the Levitical code – anyone who is 'defiled' could not take part in religious worship.[11] Homosexuality is no more singled out as a special case deserving condemnation than mixing cotton and wool in the same garment. It is our modern assumptions that enable us to stress the one and reject the other. There were many things that were considered as 'dirty' – particularly anything relating to bodily orifices. If anything, heterosexual sex was an exception to the general 'dirtiness' associated with periods, wet dreams or sex in general, and it is for this reason that homosexuality was condemned, as well as for its association with pagan religions. The Levitical purity code describes homosexual acts as 'something revolting', clearly showing the purity basis of the prohibition.

---

[8] Leviticus 19:19.
[9] Leviticus 18:23.
[10] Deuteronomy 22:5.
[11] Mary Douglas's book, *Purity and Danger*, Routledge, 1966, is the classic study in this area.

b) The New Testament

The New Testament rejects the Old Testament idea of ritual purity on which most of the traditional Jewish prohibitions had been built. However, this rejection was not a reason for imposing a new set of purity 'rules'. Indeed, Jesus showed a marked reluctance to impose such rules and had a healthy contempt for the preoccupations of the Pharisees and others with the minutiae of rules which had distorted God's relationship with human beings. The New Testament, in fact, never appeals to purity rules as a basis for any moral guidance. This poses a challenge to many Churches which have, effectively, laid down new purity laws of their own, in some cases based on Aristotle's philosophy (as we have seen in the case of Catholic Natural Law).

Homosexuality is condemned in the New Testament, although Robin Scorggs is among a number of scholars who maintain that these injunctions are not relevant for today.[12] The main thrust of his argument is that the injunctions against homosexuality are directed against exploitative sex with young boys, which was common in the Graeco-Roman world, and this has nothing to do with voluntary homosexual or lesbian relationships between adults. Roman writers tended to accept that most humans are attracted both to their own sex and to the opposite sex. Countryman says:

> The idea of the homosexual person as one who is exclusively and predominately attracted to members of the same sex appears to have been unknown to them.[13]

The modern idea of homosexuality, therefore, is totally different from the one prevailing at the time the gospels were written, just as the understanding of usury today is totally different from biblical times. It is unreasonable, therefore, to expect any biblical text to have a direct relation to the present day.

---

[12] Robin Scorggs, *The New Testament and Homosexuality: Contextual background for Contemporary Debate*, Fortress Press, 1983.
[13] Countryman, *Dirt, Greed and Sex*, p. 118.

Crucial to the claim that there is a New Testament view on homosexuality are two passages from St Paul.

i) Romans 1:21–31

… although they knew God, they did not honour him as God or give thanks to him, but they became futile in their thinking, and their senseless minds were darkened. Claiming to be wise, they became fools, and exchanged the glory of the immortal God for images resembling mortal man or birds or animals or reptiles.

Therefore God also gave them up in the lusts of their hearts to impurity, to the dishonouring of their bodies among themselves, because they exchanged the truth about God for a lie and worshipped and served the creature rather than the Creator, who is blessed for ever. Amen!

For this reason God gave them up to dishonourable passions. Their women exchanged natural relations for unnatural, and the men likewise gave up natural relations with women and were consumed with passion for one another, men committing shameless acts with men and receiving in their own persons the due penalty for their error.

And since they did not see fit to acknowledge God, God gave them up to a base mind and to improper conduct. They were filled with all manner of wickedness, evil, covetousness, malice. Full of envy, murder, strife, deceit, malignity, they are gossips, slanderers, haters of God, insolent, haughty, boastful, inventors of evil, disobedient to parents, foolish, faithless, heartless, ruthless.

The first point to recognize is that although the New Testament has been said to reject the Old Testament idea of purity, St Paul is here appealing quite specifically to the purity ideal. He is saying that homosexual acts are disordered as they are 'against nature' – they are examples of impurity since they go against the order of things 'as they ought to be'. It is, therefore a passage which is at odds with the rest of the New Testament. Countryman summarizes this passage as follows:

> Idolatry was the root sin of Gentile culture. In the creation, God left ample evidence of his goodness, power and divinity, so that any people should have known enough to worship and give thanks to him alone. The Gentiles, in the stupidity of their hearts, chose instead to worship 'a likeness of an image of a perishable human being and of birds and vermin' (Romans 1:23).[14]

If one looks at this passage as a whole it is somewhat strange, as it seems to imply that God has caused or imposed sinfulness on non-Jews as a result of their idolatry. Yet this very notion is foreign to the modern idea of human freedom and autonomy. Also, Paul seems to see some punishment being visited on those who engage in homosexual behaviour – he may have been referring to some sexually transmitted diseases which, at the time he was writing, were known to be common in some societies.[15] However, this passage cannot be used simply as a prohibition of certain sorts of behaviour – it is, rather, a return to the idea of the Gentiles as those who are outside the 'saved', who are impure or 'dirty'. How is this to be understood?

Paul starts his Letter to the Romans with what appears to be a negative attitude to Gentiles and an effective assertion of the superiority of the Jews as Christians. This contradicts the stance that Paul himself took at the Council of Jerusalem in 49 AD when he stood up for the rights of Gentile Christians to be treated equally with Jewish Christians and rejected any idea that Gentiles had first to become Jews. However, Paul is writing this letter to a particular audience – and it was almost certainly a Jewish audience living in Rome. Christianity took initial root in many Jewish communities,

[14] Countryman, *Dirt, Greed and Sex*, p. 110.
[15] Romans 1:27.

but spread rapidly amongst Gentiles and the divisions between Jewish and Gentile Christians was one of the main causes of dissension in the early Church. Paul, in his letter, is trying to win the sympathy of his Jewish audience by condemning the dirtiness or lack of purity of the Gentiles. Once he has got his audience on his side, he turns the debate round and shows that Jews, also, are far from sinless and any Jew who condemns Gentiles for lack of purity condemns himself as well.

However, Paul had an obvious problem, because he was a passionate advocate of Gentiles being fully accepted as Christians without being required to become Jews. He would not, therefore, have condemned any Gentile practice which all Gentiles would have shared as he would then have alienated his Gentile audience. Paul's strategy has to be understood, therefore, in the light of his two concerns:

a) To get his Jewish readers on his side so that they felt superior over 'impure' Gentiles.
b) Not to alienate his Gentile readers.

Once Paul's approach is recognized, his approach becomes more understandable. He condemns Gentile homosexuality (Gentiles were, of course, largely Romans and Greeks, both of whom largely accepted homosexuality) knowing that this condemnation would be readily accepted by his Jewish readers. However, he also knows that most Gentile Christians would feel superior to Gentiles who engaged in homosexual acts so they would not identify themselves with his attack. Paul was a very subtle writer!

Paul's main thrust in many places in his letters is to reject the purity ethic on which much of the Jewish Torah was based. He knew that Jesus had rejected this ethic and had sought to liberate people from the insider/outsider distinction. As referred to above, he actually travelled to Jerusalem to 'do battle' with Peter and the Jewish Christians at the first Council of the Christian Church, and his views prevailed. Why, then, should he strongly condemn in the first chapter of Romans one of the breaches of the purity laws laid down in the book of Leviticus (which included certain sorts of food, food offered to idols, those who were not circumcised and also homosexuality)? Countryman points out that this can only make sense in one of two ways:

a) If Paul considered that purity rules applied in the sexual arena but not in the area of food.
b) If Paul's condemnation of homosexuality was a rhetorical device intended only to serve Paul's wider end.

There is no evidence whatsoever for (a) in any of Paul's writings, and if this idea had been present, then all the other sexual rules set out in Leviticus would have applied as well – yet they were not. By contrast, (b) makes great sense in the context of his whole approach. The likelihood of (b) is increased when Paul's idea of homosexuality as being a punishment visited by God on non-believing Gentiles is taken into account. If this is right, then the first chapter of Romans cannot be looked on as a condemnation of homosexuality – it is rather a means used by Paul to get Jewish Christians to look to their own sinfulness rather than condemning Gentiles.

ii) 1 Corinthians 6:9–10

> Do you not know that the unrighteous will not inherit the kingdom of God? Do not be deceived. Neither the immoral, nor idolaters, nor adulterers, nor *malakoi*, nor *arsenokoitai*, nor thieves, nor the greedy, nor drunkards, nor revilers, nor robbers will inherit the kingdom of God.

Countryman points out that Paul's letters were written in Greek and what the Greek words mean when translated is not clear. The two contentious Greek words are *malakoi* (sometimes translated as homosexuality or sexual perverts) and *arsenkoitai* (translated sodomy but formed from the Greek words 'male' and 'lie'). If these words are correctly translated, it would be reasonable to expect that the words would mean much the same, as the act of homosexuality and of sodomy are closely related. John Boswell maintains that *malakoi* may have nothing to do with sexual activity at all and, even if it does, it may mean something like masturbation and that it may have been a term referring to male prostitutes.[16] *Arsenokitai* only appears in one other place in the New Testament (1 Timothy 1:10), where it comes between 'fornicators' and 'kidnappers' and there is really no clear evidence from other sources what it means. In later Christian writings the word does indeed refer to homosexuality, but it's translation in St Paul remains uncertain. To rely on such uncertain a translation for a view of what God wishes in the sexual area demands, at the least, caution – although other writers maintain that St Paul is indeed referring to homosexuality, that he condemns it and that he does consider it infringes purity rules in a way in which eating unclean food does not.

Even if Paul is referring to homosexuality and condemning it (and the weight of the argument may point in this direction) this does not mean that this view should be accepted today. Paul was a man of his time – his thought was profound and inspired but could also be mistaken. As the United Reformed Church's report on homosexuality states:

> ... when someone argues that homosexual practice must be wrong because the Bible says so, or because it is unnatural, or against creation, but would not argue in the same way that women must wear hats in church, for example, or against lending money at interest ... it is very probable that it is the continuing strength of the purity concept that is the underlying motive.[17]

[16] John Boswell, *Christianity, Sexual Tolerance and Homosexuality*, pp. 338–53.
[17] *Homosexuality: A Christian View*, Report of the Uniting Church Working Party on Homosexuality, p. 17.

c) Natural Law

One of the most significant influences on early thinking about homosexuality was the Jewish/Greek philosopher Philo (cf. pp. 43ff.). Philo was clear-cut in his condemnation of homosexuality. The reason for his attitude, and similar approaches to many sexual ideas, lay in the ideas of fertility common at the time.

It must be appreciated that it is only in the last two hundred years that the human reproductive process has been understood. Prior to that, male semen was considered to contain the whole of the new person. The male implanted a 'homunculus' in the 'nest' of the woman's womb – it was like a seed planted in a field, and the field contributed nothing to the make-up of the new individual. It followed from this that planting seed in an unsuitable field (for instance when a woman has a period) or in a place where it cannot grow (by a man having sex with another man) or by wasting seed (in masturbation) would all be wrong acts. Philo condemned homosexuality for this reason – it is much the same as sowing seed in a desert.[18] He also likens having sex with a menstruating woman to sowing barley seed in a swamp.[19] Following this logic, he goes on to say that a man who enters into a marriage with a woman he knows to be barren must be acting from selfish motives as he must be seeking pleasure alone since no conception can result from his sexual acts.[20] In fact, Philo considers sex within marriage between a husband and a wife who cannot conceive to be as wrong as homosexual acts. Philo's logic, based on the contemporary understanding of human biology, is impeccable. However, we now know that the biological basis of this position is totally false – this, therefore, means that the foundation on which Philo's position was built crumbles. As we have previously seen, there are similar assumptions made in the Aristotelian/Thomist approach to homosexuality and if these are rejected then this approach, also, can be challenged. Other criteria must, therefore, be employed.

[18] Philo, *Special Laws* 3:39–40.
[19] Philo, *Special Laws* 3:32–33.
[20] Philo, *Special Laws* 3:34–36.

Another motive for Philo's approach referred to by Countryman may have been that at the time Philo was writing, Jews were not simply living in Palestine, they were scattered over the Greek and Roman world.[21] It was essential for them to retain their identity through their religious practices and moral outlooks and they tended, therefore, to emphasize those aspects which marked them out from the prevailing culture. The Greeks, and to a lesser extent the Romans, considered homosexuality quite acceptable, and Jewish thinkers may have reacted against this. Whereas previously this had been a minor issue, it became much more important as it was one of a number of ways of demarcating Jew and Gentile.

No mention has so far been made of female homosexuality or lesbian behaviour. This was not addressed by any of the ancient thinkers and there may be various reasons for this:

a) The understanding of the human reproductive process set out above maintains that the woman has no part in the creation of a new human being except to act as a nest or field in which the embryo can grow. It follows that as lesbian behaviour does not involve the waste of any semen, so it does not involve waste of what is essentially a new human being.

b) It may be that the male theologians and philosophers who dominated intellectual life in the early years of the Christian era simply did not consider the issue of lesbian behaviour – rather like Queen Victoria!

However, the intellectual basis exists within Philo and the writings of other Jewish/Greek philosophers to condemn lesbian as well as male homosexual activity. As we have seen, Philo was heavily influenced by Plato – indeed he is sometimes described as the Jewish Plato. Both Plato and Philo were against the pursuit of pleasure as an aim – they thought that pleasure and passion were the great moral evils which had to be avoided at all costs (seventeenth-century

[21] Countryman, *Dirt, Greed and Sex*, p. 61.

puritans and their modern descendants take a similar view). This was partly due to Plato's dualist view of human beings (cf. pp. 47ff.) which emphasized the immaterial soul and regarded the body as merely the vehicle in which the soul lived. Since pleasure was concerned with the body, it would restrict the development of the soul. Philo maintained that the basis of all the virtues is self-control.[22] To the extent that male or female homosexual behaviour had pleasure as an end, it would therefore be condemned – along with all other pleasures directly associated with the body.

Philo's ideas were to influence Augustine, and Thomas Aquinas was to give philosophic expression to them using the philosophy of Aristotle (cf. chapter 6). These ideas dominated European thought until comparatively recently.

d) The Nineteenth and Twentieth Centuries

In the nineteenth century, homosexuality was considered as a mental illness, and many of those who practised homosexuality were locked up in appalling conditions in mental institutions. A law was passed declaring homosexual practice to be an 'act of gross indecency'. Churches uniformly condemned homosexual practice in the strongest terms. As Dr Iain Frew points out, the result was great secrecy and the risk of blackmail and isolation. The medical profession was no help at all – in fact they introduced an operation called frontal leucotomy which involved:

> ... opening the skull and cutting the nerve pathways from the frontal lobes to the rest of the brain ... The operation in effect destroyed the patient's personality to a major degree; some patients became little better than zombies. A more cruel, mutilating, and pointless exercise would be hard to imagine.[23]

[22] Philo, *The Contemplative Life* 34.
[23] Dr Iain Frew in *Homosexuality: A Christian View.*

Those who practised homosexuality (but not, interestingly, lesbians who largely were tolerated or ignored – possibly because males could not or would not imagine lesbian practices) continued to be persecuted and prosecuted. The trial and imprisonment of Oscar Wilde was one of the best-known instances. Imprisonment in an all-male gaol in fact increased the number of homosexual acts as male rape was (and still is today) common in prison. If one wanted to alter homosexual behaviour then it would be hard to imagine a more ludicrous way of attempting to do this than by locking homosexuals up with an exclusively male prison population. Prisons can provide an indicator to the variability of sexual activity as, in all male and all female prisons, 'same sex' sexual activity may occur between participants who would previously have been exclusively heterosexual.

The 1957 Wolfenden report marked a turning point in attitudes, as it recognized, for the first time, that homosexual inclination was something innate. In particular, it called for the abandonment of attempts to alter homosexual behaviour, but the report was in advance of public opinion and it has taken nearly 40 years for attitudes to homosexuality to begin to change.

The advent of AIDS which affected the homosexual community particularly badly (because the AIDS virus is more readily transmitted in male homosexual sex than in heterosexual activity) led to many of the latent prejudices against homosexual behaviour surfacing once more, particularly in the United States. Some Christians described AIDS as being sent by God as a punishment of homosexuals, although others showed great compassion and understanding.

Some have reported 'success' in 'curing' those who practised same-sex sexual activity and getting them to pursue a heterosexual lifestyle, but the evidence is clear that almost all such people are bisexual (being attracted to both men and women) and they have merely been 'encouraged' to pursue one aspect of their sexuality and not the other. Many homosexuals feel rejected and marginalized by the attitudes of society and religious leaders, and although changes are slowly being made, many people still suffer from a high degree of ignorance and prejudice.

e) Homosexuality Today

Many people still find homosexual acts abhorrent and repulsive – this may well stem from their background and education and it may be due to feeling personally threatened by these tendencies which, research has shown, are present in many human beings, albeit in latent form.

The climate of disapproval toward male homosexual and lesbian behaviour is, however, changing, and it is significant than in an extended survey of the attitudes of British young people, only 18 per cent of females and 34 per cent of males considered that male homosexual acts were morally wrong whilst 18 per cent of females and 22 per cent of males considered sexual acts between lesbians to be morally wrong.[24] (The greater prejudice of males in both categories is noteworthy.)

What, then, should a modern moral position be if it is based, as suggested in chapter 11, on an appraisal of human nature which takes into account the physical and psychological data now available to us? In any discussion of the moral issue of male homosexual or lesbian issues, a clear separation has been made between:

a) A physical inclination to a member of the same sex which may be due to genetics or experiences in childhood, and
b) The physical expression of this inclination in sexual acts.

As we have seen, Natural Law distinguishes between these, maintaining that the first is a defect – but in no sense a moral defect. A disordered inclination is not morally worse than having defective eyesight or the lack of a full head of hair. We cannot help our

---

[24] For detailed figures, see the appendix.

inclinations and if our natural inclinations are not heterosexual then there is no moral fault involved. However, as soon as a man or woman gives expression to this 'defective' inclination, this is considered to be a free act which must be morally condemned. Although this is the official Catholic position, this does not mean that this distinction is always accepted in practice, and there is still great suspicion of those with a homosexual or lesbian inclination by those who consider themselves 'normal' because they are heterosexual. This often leads to a condemnation of the inclination ((a) above) even when it is not expressed. It is for this reason, for instance, that priests and nuns who are gay are encouraged not to say anything publicly about their inclination because of provoking scandal.

Fr William McDonough, Professor of moral theology and spiritual formation at the St Paul Seminary School of Divinity in the US, argues that the acknowledged homosexual orientation of gay celibate priests is a gift to the Catholic Church. Indeed he maintains that Catholic magisterial teaching, which sees sexuality as a fundamental characteristic of being human, 'provides the logic for acknowledging gay celibacy'.[25] His claim is that there is a conspiracy of silence between Catholic priests and their bishops to the effect that priests who are homosexual do not acknowledge their inclination as to do so might provoke a scandal in an American society which, in the majority, disapproves of homosexuality. This attitude betrays a form of insincerity, since, as we have seen, the Catholic Church does not consider that a homosexual or lesbian inclination is morally evil – these only become morally evil when they are given genital expression. McDonough maintains that:

a general acknowledgement, in both public and personal form, of the existence of gay priestly celibacy is a timely way to affect the broader culture.[26]

[25] William McDonough, 'Acknowledging the Gift of Gay Priestly Celibacy', *Review for Religious* 55 (1996).
[26] McDonough, p. 294.

In other words he maintains that if Catholic priests (and the same applies to many Anglican and other celibate bishops, priests and nuns) could be honest about their sexual orientation, even if they are celibate and this inclination is not practised, this would have a beneficial effect on society as a whole, as those with a homosexual or lesbian inclination could acknowledge this inclination without facing moral censure. Many priests repress their sexual inclination and throw themselves into good works and priestly activity to conceal from themselves that they are denying an essential part of their humanity. Andrew Sullivan says of such priests:

> You dream grandiose dreams, construct a fantasy of a future, power your energies into some massive distraction, pursue a consoling career to cover up the lie at the centre of your existence.[27]

If priests and nuns could find the courage to openly acknowledge that they are sexual beings, then this might show their parishioners that to be human is to be sexual and that a sexual orientation is perfectly normal. It might also be a witness to their parishioners that a homosexual or lesbian inclination is not something to be ashamed of – and that the issue is how this inclination is used. It does not follow, of course, that any sexual inclination, whether hetero- or homosexual, is actually practised, but there are few rounded people who can deny that they are sexual beings. To refuse to accept this, to suppress and distort it, is effectively to suppress part of our humanity. The refusal to face up to the reality of homosexual and lesbian inclination and to allow it to be openly acknowledged represents a moral failure by the Catholic Church as it is part of this Church's own teaching that such inclinations are not morally evil. It represents, in effect, an unwillingness to stand openly for what is believed to be right in order to placate the majority of Catholic congregations who might find the official position 'unacceptable'.

[27] Andrew Sullivan, *Virtually Normal*, p. 190.

None of this, however, addresses the second question – whether it can be morally right for homosexual or lesbian inclinations ever to be given physical sexual expression. The evidence today that some people are sexually attracted to members of the same sex rather than to the opposite sex is overwhelming. Even if the argument that a heterosexual inclination is the norm is accepted, this does not get away from the clear fact that many people are not heterosexual. Are they, then, to suppress all sexual desire, all opportunity to physically express their love, and to be denied the ability to be close to another human being in a way which is natural to them? To maintain this is tantamount to claiming that a person who has no arms due to a birth defect should not be allowed to write with their feet (as some do) because this is 'unnatural'. Such an argument today verges on the absurd.

Casual homosexual or lesbian sexual activity indulged in solely for the pleasure of the act rather than as a manifestation of a relationship can be as destructive and as meaningless and as damaging to the human integrity of those involved as casual heterosexual sex. In previous chapters, the dangers of seeing another human being purely in terms of his or her function have been outlined and also the emphasis has been placed on 'mystery' involved in two people giving themselves to each other in love and intimacy. However, this 'giving', this intimate sharing, is as possible between two women or between two men as it is between a man and a woman. Workers in AIDS hospitals sometimes say that the love, commitment, gentleness, dedication and concern expressed by the homosexual partners of those dying of AIDS are greater than anything they have seen between heterosexual couples. Jesus emphasized the importance of love and friendship – a traditional Christian chant, made popular once again by the monks of Taizé Abbey, says:

Ubi caritas et amor, Deus ibi est.

'Wherever compassion and love is present, there God is found.' If genuine, deep and committed love is possible between males and between females, then there seems no moral reason why this love should not be expressed sexually if the circumstances as well as the depth and commitment of the relationship warrants this. Essentially, there seems no difference between heterosexuals, homosexuals and lesbians in this respect. The key issue is the depth and commitment of the relationship, as well as one's other commitments, rather than the act itself.

This is, of course, to reject a deontological approach which sees acts in themselves as being disordered and instead to maintain that acts are morally right or wrong depending on the context or situation in which they are performed. A man who cuts a woman's stomach may be attempting to kill her or to perform a life-saving operation – only the context will determine the kind of act and also its moral worth.

Peter Gomes, Professor of Christian moral philosophy at Harvard University, argues that although the biblical writers do condemn homosexual behaviour, nevertheless they:

> never contemplated a form of homosexuality in which loving, homogeneous and faithful persons sought to live out the implications of the gospel with as much fidelity to it as any heterosexual believer.[28]

The Catholic Church, in the Second Vatican Council (1965), has moved to say that the purpose of sex is both procreative and unitive – even though at present it rejects any separation of these two. It may be (although some more conservative Catholic scholars disagree with this), that it is possible that the Catholic Church, in the next century, may follow the Anglican and most Protestant Churches in separating these two purposes, opening the door to artificial means of birth control. Once this separation takes place it could, and there is no necessity here, lead to a reconsideration of the unitive role of sexual activity between members of the same sex.

---

[28] Peter Gomes, *The Good Book*, William Morrow, 1997.

Other Churches, including the Anglican, Methodist and United Reformed, are wrestling with the issue of homosexual activity both among lay people and clergy. This wrestling often involves passionately-held convictions and strong feelings and, sadly, is sometimes based more on prejudice than on careful analysis. At the least, these matters demand careful deliberation and the recognition that simple answers are often based on inadequate consideration of the complexity of the issues.

NINETEEN
The Outsiders

There are many outsiders in our society and many who consider themselves as outsiders because of their sexual behaviour. Those who masturbate, who have sex before marriage, who commit adultery or who are practising male homosexuals or lesbians may well be made to feel outsiders by certain more conventional groups – although in some cases what was previously considered the behaviour of 'the outsider' is now considered as the norm – those who have sex before marriage are good examples. The moral issues confronting these groups have been discussed. However, there are other categories of people who may be considered much more 'unacceptable', including those who use the services of prostitutes; prostitutes themselves; paedophiles or those who enjoy looking at pictures of young children; the rapist (both within and outside marriage); those who combine sex with violence; those with graphic sexual fantasies and others. Each of these groups, and the many different individuals within them, deserve fuller treatment than is possible here.

The person who uses the services of a prostitute will often do so because he (it is usually a male) is unable to sustain any long-term, intimate loving relationship with another person. The causes of this may be many and various, but the visits he makes will usually be a symptom of a deeper disorder and lack of wholeness which needs to be met with love and understanding rather than condemnation. Real love for and by another may enable and strengthen the person and its lack may weaken and dehumanize. The only real experience of human contact some people obtain may be in sexual acts which, in themselves, are superficial by the standards set out in this book – but these actions can be humanizing and life-giving, although they can also be dehumanizing and degrading. The same can apply to some of the other groups mentioned, although a distinction must be drawn between situations where the two people involved are both willing partners and situations where one person exercises dominance and coercive power over another (for instance in paedophilia or the abuse of those who are in a position where, emotionally, psychologically or physically, they are unable to resist). The man who uses a prostitute is at least paying for her or his services which may be given more or less voluntarily, whilst the rapist and paedophile are both using their power to subjugate, debase and abuse others and are in a different category. Even in these cases, however, there may be deeper psychological reasons which, whilst they may not excuse the behaviour, can help to make it more understandable.

It has been said that 'to understand is to forgive', and certainly any who have worked actively in the field of psychological analysis or counselling will know that the histories of those with sexual problems are usually complicated and that they will often need help rather than condemnation. Most 'sex offenders' in prison are damaged, hurt and deeply vulnerable people – however much hurt and damage they themselves may have brought into the lives of others. Few of us are entirely 'normal', whatever that means, and if we are in this fortunate position then we may well have a great deal to be thankful for in terms of a happy, secure and balanced childhood in which we could grow into adults who are capable of both giving and receiving love. Not everyone, however, is in this position.

Jesus went out to all those who were least accepted in the society in which he lived. He had friends who were tax collectors, who were loathed and despised because they were almost always corrupt and worked for the hated Roman authorities; who were women, who were not accepted in traditional Jewish society as equal companions for a man, however highly they were valued in the home; who were prostitutes, lepers, outcasts and failures. Few women choose prostitution as a deliberate choice when other options are available – many are driven to prostitution having been thrown out by their families, by not having a roof over their heads, by desperation and need and, in some cases, by the need to support loved ones. In some cases they may be driven down this route by inner feelings of worthlessness which can be traced back to when they were abused, either sexually or psychologically, at an early age.

Central to Jesus' message was that God unconditionally loved every human being and that this love is not conditional on 'being good'. This love cannot be earned, and no matter what human beings do, they cannot prevent God's love being available to them. Jesus taught that God would unconditionally forgive anyone who showed any sign of wanting to come to him and that real love always forgives. He was quick to condemn those religious leaders who were sure of their own sanctity and those who were cold and indifferent but he was always unconditionally available to those who were weak and vulnerable.

In many cases, the weakest and most vulnerable human beings are those who have difficulty in accepting themselves and their sexuality, and these are the people to whom the Church, if it is following Christ, should show the most love, commitment and understanding. Sadly, but frequently:

- The Church often reacts in the opposite manner being cold, harsh and indifferent to the vulnerable humanity exhibited in our sexuality.
- Too often it is the proud priests, so sure of their moral rectitude, who will condemn the outsider or the sexually deviant,
- Too often it is the secure, apparently happily married or celibate churchgoer who will reject those whose norms of behaviour are regarded as unacceptable whilst they themselves are only too willing to compromise on issues of social justice and care for the marginalized.

Yet, in the poverty and weakness of those at the bottom of the human pile (at least to the world's way of looking at things), can often be found the gentleness, understanding, compassion and love that are the marks of God's presence. All human beings are sexual, it is an essential part of our common human nature. Dealing with the challenges posed by our sexual natures will never be easy and the complexities cannot be captured in a simple set of rules. However, to deny our sexual natures or to use other people for our own sexual gratification against their will must always be wrong.

All human beings are travellers – we are all on the road to somewhere. For those with religious belief, this 'somewhere' may be towards God, for others it may be expressed as a search for truth, whilst to others it will be a matter of becoming more fully human. For many people, there is a day by day attempt to survive in a hostile world and each new dawn marks an achievement, another step forward on what appears to be a grim road leading to nowhere but despair. Perhaps all roads, however, lead towards the same destination – to be fully human requires a search for truth and truth may be intimately connected with God. All human beings start at different points on this journey – some have come from happy, united homes where they were able to come to terms with their sexuality and to learn to engage in adult relationships. Others may have found their lives distorted by their past experiences. None of us can or should condemn others. Our task is to progress on the one road and, as we do so, to help our fellow travellers with care, compassion and understanding. We cannot and must not be content with our own progress on the road but we must not reject others whom we may (perhaps mistakenly) think are less far advanced.

This book has attempted to chart a way forward in the field of sexual morality by pointing to those features of our shared humanity that are conducive to human life and wholeness. It has argued that the foundations for many present attitudes to sexuality are flimsy, but has maintained that the search for a true understanding of our humanity and how our sexual natures should be expressed is a worthy endeavour. It has resisted giving simplistic solutions yet has affirmed the mystery and depth involved in human intimacy. Perhaps it has also pointed to the need to be gentle with ourselves and with one another as we grapple with difficult problems, and to see that the presence of genuine, deep and committed love, humility, compassion and gentleness provide the best signs of God's presence – and this presence may be found in the most unexpected places.

Questions for Discussion

1   Answer the questions listed in the appendix and explain your reasons for your answers.

2   Examine the answers to the questions in the appendix. Do you notice any difference in attitudes between boys and girls or those who believe in God and those who do not? Suggest reasons.

3   Do you consider that there are any moral problems associated with cybersex? Explain and justify your answer.

4   What are the arguments for and against the use of virtual reality techniques in the sexual sphere? Explain your views on this issue.

5   Set out your understanding of what it means to marry someone.

6   Some young people who are lonely and unhappy feel that marriage will overcome their problems. Do you agree? Give your reasons.

7   What would it mean to have an intimate friend who was a 'soul mate'? Could one have such a friend of the opposite sex if one was married?

8   Can it ever be morally right for a husband or wife to have secrets from their partner? Give examples and your reasons.

9   Do you consider that divorce can be morally acceptable given that permanent vows were made on marriage? Suggest reasons which would support and reasons which would challenge your view.

10 Can it be morally right to make lifelong vows to someone in a second marriage when the first marriage partner (to whom the person may have made similar vows) is still living?

11 What do you see as the major advantages of celibacy today? Has the celibate life any relevance?

12 If you had to bring up children in the modern world and give them advice on sexual ethics, what principles would you rely on to provide guidance? Give reasons for your answer.

Postscript

Many will disagree with the arguments in this book. Their basis for doing so will probably be drawn from one of the following and it is worth setting out the challenge they face. If this book's arguments are rejected by:

1 **Appeal to Natural Law**, then clear physiological and psychological evidence needs to be given for exactly what this nature 'should' be. It must then be shown how those who are considered to be 'defective' because they do not have this stated nature should then behave and why.

2 **Appeal to the Bible or some other holy text**, then it must be shown on what basis some texts are shown to apply today and others are not, and the findings of the latest scholarship must also be addressed.

3 **Appeal to the teaching authority of a particular religious group**, then it must be shown why this teaching authority should be accepted on sexual matters today when so often in the past religious groups have been shown to be grievously mistaken.

4 **Appeal to the duty involved, say, in marriage vows**, then argument must be put forward why these vows and the sexual obligations they are held to entail should be maintained when love has declined or disappeared and when one party may be abusing another or preventing the other's human development.

5 **Appeal to personal conviction**, then it must be explained

why one person's convictions must be accepted when so many disagree with him or her.

6 **Appeal to the view of a particular community**, then it must be shown why these views are valid when there are many alternatives or whether it is being asserted that conformity is the highest value.

On a more positive note, any alternative account must also demonstrate why the view it upholds contributes to human well-being and wholeness and that it is life-affirming rather than life-denying.

At the least, the importance of these issues should encourage humility by those who claim to 'know the truth' and who attempt to impose it on others. Perhaps everyone – parents, children, priests, teachers and others – should be willing to be modest about their certainties, whilst still engaging in the passionate search for truth.

Survey Results

In 1996/7 a survey was undertaken among over 3000 British 16–18-year-olds across England and Scotland, asking about their views of morality in the sexual arena. Those survyed were asked to indicate whether they considered themselves to belong to the religious groups named. Separate headings were given for Muslims, Jews, Hindus and 'Other', but the number of responses from these groups were not large enough to be statistically significant so these are all included together under the heading 'Other Religion'.

Those questioned were asked whether they found it embarrassing to answer these questions and 95 per cent of girls and 92 per cent of boys said 'no'. They were also asked whether the issues of sexual ethics should be dealt with frankly and openly in schools between the ages of 16 to 18, and 96.5 per cent said 'yes', with a further 1.9 per cent saying 'don't know' and only 1.6 per cent saying 'no'. The results are tabulated below:

1 Do you consider that it is morally wrong to make love to someone with whom you are in a long-term loving relationship when you are not married?

	YES	NO	DON'T KNOW
Agnostic	3%	96.1%	0.9%
Atheist	1.1%	98.2%	0.7%
Anglican	14.5%	80%	5.5%
Roman Catholic	11.7%	85.4%	2.9%

	YES	NO	DON'T KNOW
Other Christian	28.9%	66.7%	4.4%
Other Religion	15%	81.1%	3.9%
Boys	12.9%	84%	3.1%
Girls	12.7%	84.1%	3.2%
Those studying theology and/or philosophy	13.7%	83.1%	3.2%
Those studying other subjects	8.1%	89.2%	2.7%

2 Do you consider that it is morally wrong to make love to someone with whom you are (a) not in a long-term relationship, provided (b) it is pleasurable; (c) the girl does not get pregnant, and (d) 'no one gets hurt'?

	YES	NO	DON'T KNOW
Agnostic	15.4%	75.2%	9.4%
Atheist	10%	81.4%	8.6%
Anglican	42.7%	45.9%	11.4%
Roman Catholic	39%	50.1%	10.9%
Other Christian	50.8%	40.4%	8.8%
Other Religion	31.3%	58.7%	10%
Boys	30%	60%	10%
Girls	33.4%	56.6%	10%
Those studying theology and/or philosophy	34.3%	55.7%	10%
Those studying other subjects	24%	66.6%	9.4%

3 Do you consider masturbation to be a morally wrong act?

	YES	NO	DON'T KNOW
Agnostic	2.8%	87.5%	9.7%
Atheist	1.8%	94.6%	3.6%
Anglican	7.4%	74.9%	17.7%
Roman Catholic	12%	72.7%	15.3%

	YES	NO	DON'T KNOW
Other Christian	12%	67.5%	20.5%
Other Religion	8.9%	74.1%	17%
Boys	10.2%	79.5%	10.3%
Girls	6.4%	77.7%	15.9%
Those studying theology and/or philosophy	7.6%	77.4%	15%
Those studying other subjects	5.6%	82.5%	11.9%

4 Assume two people are in a long-term relationship and they are sleeping together. If one of the two goes on holiday with a large group which does not include his or her partner, would it be morally right to sleep with someone on holiday provided he or she has told his/her partner that he/she is 'going single' whilst away?

	YES	NO	DON'T KNOW
Agnostic	24.9%	63.2%	11.9%
Atheist	32.1%	55.4%	12.5%
Anglican	22%	71.6%	6.4%
Roman Catholic	21%	72.7%	6.3%
Other Christian	19.6%	74%	6.4%
Other Religion	25.1%	63.3%	11.6%
Boys	27.2%	63.2%	9.6%
Girls	22.1%	69.3%	8.6%
Those studying theology and/or philosophy	22.9%	67.9%	9.2%
Those studying other subjects	25.6%	67.3%	7.1%

5   Do you consider that the use of artificial means of birth control (the pill, condoms, etc.) by a healthy couple is always morally wrong?

	YES	NO	DON'T KNOW
Agnostic	0.7%	98%	1.3%
Atheist	1.7%	97.6%	0.7%
Anglican	1%	98.9%	0.2%
Roman Catholic	5.8%	91.9%	2.3%
Other Christian	1.7%	96.2%	2.1%
Other Religion	5.4%	91.9%	2.7%
Boys	4.2%	94.3%	1.5%
Girls	1.6%	96.9%	1.5%
Those studying theology and/or philosophy	2.2%	96.3%	1.5%
Those studying other subjects	2.5%	96.2%	1.3%

6   Do you consider that the 'morning after pill' (which may involve preventing the fertilized egg implanting in the womb) is morally worse than a barrier method of contraception (such as the condom)?

	YES	NO	DON'T KNOW
Agnostic	33.4%	60.5%	6.1%
Atheist	22.8%	70.4%	6.8%
Anglican	44.3%	46.7%	9%
Roman Catholic	47.8%	40.8%	11.4%
Other Christian	44.6%	45.9%	9.5%
Other Religion	36.4%	54.7%	8.9%
Boys	33%	57%	10%
Girls	41.5%	50.6%	7.9%
Those studying theology and/or philosophy	41.2%	50%	8.8%
Those studying other subjects	27.3%	66%	6.7%

7 Do you consider that there are any circumstances that could make adultery morally right?

	YES	NO	DON'T KNOW
Agnostic	42%	40.3%	17.7%
Atheist	50%	35.4%	14.6%
Anglican	29.6%	59.1%	11.3%
Roman Catholic	30.4%	57.1%	12.5%
Other Christian	24%	65.3%	10.7%
Other Religion	36.3%	49.4%	14.3%
Boys	37%	51%	12%
Girls	33.5%	52.5%	14.1%
Those studying theology and/or philosophy	34.9%	51.5%	13.1%
Those studying other subjects	31.9%	55%	13.1%

8 Do you consider sex between lesbians to be always morally wrong?

	YES	NO	DON'T KNOW
Agnostic	8%	85.3%	6.7%
Atheist	7.1%	90.4%	2.5%
Anglican	22.8%	62.3%	14.9%
Roman Catholic	17.1%	66.3%	16.6%
Other Christian	39.1%	49.2%	11.7%
Other Religion	18.2%	73%	8.8%
Boys	22.4%	68.6%	9%
Girls	18.4%	70.3%	11.3%
Those studying theology and/or philosophy	19.1%	70%	10.9%
Those studying other subjects	20.2%	70%	9.8%

9 Do you consider sex between male homosexuals to be always morally wrong?

	YES	NO	DON'T KNOW
Agnostic	11.8%	81.5%	6.7%
Atheist	10.4%	87.1%	2.5%
Anglican	25.5%	59.9%	14.6%
Roman Catholic	19.7%	62.9%	17.4%
Other Christian	42.6%	46.2%	11.2%
Other Religion	23.6%	67.6%	17.4%
Boys	34.3%	56.6%	9.1%
Girls	18.9%	70%	11.1%
Those studying theology and/or philosophy	22.1%	70%	11%
Those studying other subjects	26.7%	94.1%	9.2%

The survey was conducted by asking A-level students aged 16–18 attending Sixth Form RE conferences throughout England and in Scotland to complete a questionnaire. The results were confidential and were not seen by their teachers. Although the size of the survey makes the results statistically highly significant, its limitations include:

a) The survey was amongst the more intelligent children in the country since these children are undertaking post–16 study.

b) Many of those attending were studying RE/Philosophy and the differences between those studying these subjects and others are set out in the results.

c) No account is taken of any students who did not wish to complete the questionnaire and although it is believed that the number of these is very small (confirmed by the questionnaire asking whether those responding found it embarrassing to answer – to which 94.5 per cent said 'no'), this cannot be proved.

Two important points need to be made: a) What people consider is morally right is not, of course, the same as what *is* morally right – but at the least these figures are significant in showing the gulf between traditional teaching on many areas of sexual morality and the views of young people today. Some may hold that this is due to them being morally debased or, more positively, it may be due to them having recognized features of human nature which have not always been recognized by theologians and philosophers in the past. It may also be due to a wide range of other factors; and b) The fact that young people do or do not consider certain actions to be morally right or wrong does not mean that they themselves would do these actions. This distinction is important.

Index

Abraham 18ff
abuse 113ff, 162, 222, 223
Adam 5ff, 111, 139
adultery 12, 33, 39, 53, 59, 82,
    120, 187ff
AIDS 215, 219
anima/animus 110
animals 15, 119, 122, 160, 205
annulment of marriage 69–70
Aquinas, St Thomas 48, 59, 60ff,
    82–3, 93, 95, 117, 159
Augustine, St 14, 15, 52, 53–7, 74,
    75, 81, 83, 93, 159, 163, 189

Basil of Caesarea 52
Bathsheba 27ff
biblical development xii
Boswell, John 211
Brown, Peter 49–50

Cahill, Lisa 9, 80–82
Callaghan, Brendan SJ 142
Casti Connubii 180
celibacy 47, 53, 63, 75, 82, 168
childhood 103ff, 114, 121, 140,
    141, 223
children 20, 35, 55, 70, 72, 83,
    109, 112, 185, 195, 196
Chrysostom, John, St 10, 76

clergy, married 75, 79, 83ff
clitoris 120, 160
cohabitation 76, 185–6
conscience 174ff
contraception 13, 61, 74ff, 155ff
Council of Trent 69
Countryman, William 29, 204,
    206ff
Cranmer 196
creation, the 3ff, 122
crowning ceremony on marriage
    71
cybersex 149ff

David, King 27ff
Decalogue, the – *see* Ten
    Commandments, the
despair 109, 116, 166
Diamond, Jared 119
divorce 38ff, 46, 69, 72, 195–9
Dominian, Jack 109, 112, 118,
    123–4, 161, 192
Donum Vitae 156–7

ego, the 105
Ephraim, man from 24ff
Erasmus 78ff
erections 54
Erikson, Erik 108, 166

238